About OKCIR

Omar Khayyam Center for Integrative Research in Utopia, Mysticism, and Science (Utopystics)

www.okcir.com

OKCIR (est. 2002) is an independent research, pedagogical, and publishing initiative dedicated to exploring, in a simultaneously world-historical and self-reflective framework, the human search for a just global society.

Since the world's utopian, mystical, and scientific movements have been the primary sources of inspiration, knowledge, and/or practice in this field, OKCIR aims to critically reexamine the shortcomings and contributions of these world-historical traditions—seeking to clearly understand why they have failed to bring about the good society, and what each can integratively contribute toward realizing that end.

The center aims to develop new conceptual (methodological, theoretical, historical), practical, pedagogical, inspirational and disseminative structures of knowledge whereby the individual can radically understand and determine how world-history and her/his selves constitute one another.

OKCIR promotes creative exercises in liberating sociology and alternative pluriversities of knowledge production and publication in the global cyberspace. As a virtual research center, its publications are available in part freely online in its open-stacks digital library, in part via subscription to its own or other academic database member-stacks, and others for purchase online via the Okcir Store and other online distributors. Selected publications are also available in print for online purchase by libraries, institutions, and interested print readers.

OKCIR pursues innovative editorial, digital, and print publishing practices reflecting its substantive goals, and is the publisher of *Human Architecture: Journal of the Sociology of Self-Knowledge* (ISSN: 1540-5699, est. 2002) which explores issues pertaining to the center's interests. *Human Architecture* is a hybrid scholarly journal whose edited and monographed issues are simultaneously published also as individual books in hardcover, softcover, and pdf and/or epub ebook formats (with separately assigned ISBNs).

Tayyebeh Series in East-West Research and Translation (2014-) and Ahead Publishing House (imprint: Okcir Press) (1991-) respectively honor Tayyebeh Tamjidi (1928-2020) and Mohammed (Ahad) Tamjidi (1930-2007) whose parental love and support made the life and works of Mohammad H. (Behrooz) Tamdgidi, the founder of OKCIR, possible.

About the Author

Mohammad H. (Behrooz) Tamdgidi, Ph.D., is the founding director and editor of OKCIR: Omar Khayyam Center for Integrative Research in Utopia, Mysticism, and Science (Utopystics) (*www.okcir.com*) and its journal, *Human Architecture: Journal of the Sociology of Self-Knowledge* (ISSN: 1540-5699), which have served since 2002 to frame his independent research, pedagogical, and publishing initiatives. Tamdgidi holds a Ph.D. and M.A. in sociology in conjunction with a graduate certificate in Middle Eastern studies from Binghamton University (SUNY). He received his B.A. in architecture from U.C. Berkeley. Other than his 12-book series currently in progress on Omar Khayyam's life, works, and poetry under the common title *Omar Khayyam's Secret: Hermeneutics of the Robaiyat in Quantum Sociological Imagination* (Okcir Press, 2021-), he has previously authored *Liberating Sociology: From Newtonian Toward Quantum Imaginations: Volume 1: Unriddling the Quantum Enigma* (Okcir Press, 2020), *Gurdjieff and Hypnosis: A Hermeneutic Study* (Palgrave Macmillan, 2009) and *Advancing Utopistics: The Three Component Parts and Errors of Marxism* (Routledge/Paradigm, 2007). Tamdgidi is a former associate professor of sociology specializing in social theory at the University of Massachusetts (UMass) Boston and has taught sociology at SUNY-Binghamton and SUNY-Oneonta. Due to research commitments facing urgent deadlines, and preferences for written communication and privacy, the author can be reached only by email.

Published to Date in the 12-Book *Omar Khayyam's Secret* Series

Omar Khayyam's Secret: Hermeneutics of the Robaiyat in Quantum Sociological Imagination: Book 1: New Khayyami Studies: Quantumizing the Newtonian Structures of C. Wright Mills's Sociological Imagination for A New Hermeneutic Method (Okcir Press, 2021)

Omar Khayyam's Secret: Hermeneutics of the Robaiyat in Quantum Sociological Imagination: Book 2: Khayyami Millennium: Reporting the Discovery and the Reconfirmation of the True Dates of Birth and Passing of Omar Khayyam (AD 1021-1123) (Okcir Press, 2021)

Omar Khayyam's Secret: Hermeneutics of the Robaiyat in Quantum Sociological Imagination: Book 3: Khayyami Astronomy: How Omar Khayyam's Newly Discovered True Birth Date Horoscope Reveals the Origins of His Pen Name and Independently Confirms His Authorship of the Robaiyat (Okcir Press, 2021)

Omar Khayyam's Secret: Hermeneutics of the Robaiyat in Quantum Sociological Imagination: Book 4: Khayyami Philosophy: The Ontological Structures of the Robaiyat in Omar Khayyam's Last Written Keepsake Treatise on the Science of the Universals of Existence (Okcir Press, 2021)

Tamám Shud

About this Report

In this OKCIR Research Report, hermeneutic sociologist, Khayyami scholar, and founding director of Omar Khayyam Center for Integrative Research (OKCIR), Mohammad H. (Behrooz) Tamdgidi, Ph.D., reports having solved the mystery of the code associated with the so-called "Somerton Man" or "Tamám Shud" case.

The mysterious code appearing on the back page of a first edition copy of Edward FitzGerald's *The Rubaiyat of Omar Khayyam*—found months following the death of The Somerton Man (TSM) in South Adelaide, Australia, on Dec. 1, 1948—was a suicide contemplation and planning note he was poetically drafting for himself in the form of a quatrain on the back of his copy of *The Rubaiyat*, giving a gist of why and how he planned to carry out a deliberately mystery-laden suicide as his last dance for a lasting life. The code was the creative DNA of his suicide plot.

It was written in the 'Tamám Shud' transliteration style—in this case not from Persian, but from Arabic with which he must have been familiar, either natively due to coming ancestrally from the ethnically diverse and widely multilingual Russian Caucasus and/or by training and education. In other words, the 'Tamám Shud' torn-out piece found in TSM's fob pocket not only served as a bread crumb lead to his suicide note, it also offered the key to the code's deciphering.

DNA is a self-replicating matter that reproduces the basic structure of a substance. TSM's 'code' offers the DNA of his last dance performance in public hoping for a lasting life, one that was sketched amid his medical suffering. He was reflecting on his life, terminal illness, and expected imminent death, while reading the meanings conveyed about life and death in FitzGerald's translation of Omar Khayyam's *Rubaiyat*—a work of art that offered TSM a practical and proven example of how one can physically die but endure in human memory and spirit forever.

This report mainly focuses on deciphering TSM's code, but the findings are also used to shed brief new light on one and/or another alternative wider story of what took place in Adelaide in 1948, in the years leading to it, and in the decades thereafter. The report invites readers to rethink the relevance of Omar Khayyam's poetry to the case, and also asks a pertinent question about another fold of the mystery, that is, why did it take so long to decipher a code that could have actually been decoded much earlier?

The Somerton Man or Tamám Shud case has important lessons for us beyond the confines of the personal troubles of a man and those he knew, inviting us to use our sociological imaginations to explore such troubles in relation to the public issues that concern us all beyond the shores of Australia, and beyond the national and disciplinary walls fragmenting our lives, universities, and scientific methods in favor of transcultural and transdisciplinary modes of inquiry.

The report ends with a dancing celebration for deciphering the code as a new window to learning the true story and possible identity of the Somerton Man.

Tamám Shud

How the Somerton Man's Last Dance
for a Lasting Life Was Decoded

Omar Khayyam Center Research Report

Mohammad H. Tamdgidi

Human Architecture: Journal of the Sociology of Self-Knowledge

Okcir Press

TAMÁM SHUD
How the Somerton Man's Last Dance for a Lasting Life Was Decoded —
Omar Khayyam Center Research Report

Author: Mohammad H. Tamdgidi

First Edition: October 1, 2021
Okcir Press • P. O. Box 393, Belmont, MA 02478, USA • www.okcir.com
For ordering or other inquiries contact: info[at]okcir.com

Okcir Press is an imprint of Ahead Publishing House, which is a division of OKCIR: Omar Khayyam Center for Integrative Research in Utopia, Mysticism, and Science (Utopystics)

Library of Congress Control Number: 2021919688

Publisher Cataloging in Publication Data

Tamám Shud: How the Somerton Man's Last Dance for a Lasting Life Was Decoded — Omar Khayyam Center Research Report / Mohammad H. Tamdgidi, 1959- / First Edition: October 1, 2021

Human Architecture: Journal of the Sociology of Self-Knowledge

100 pages • 6x9 inches • Includes references
ISBN-13: 978-1-64098-022-8 • ISBN-10: 1-64098-022-9 (hardcover : alk. paper)
ISBN-13: 978-1-64098-023-5 • ISBN-10: 1-64098-023-7 (softcover : alk. paper)
ISBN-13: 978-1-64098-024-2 • ISBN-10: 1-64098-024-5 (EPub ebook)
ISBN-13: 978-1-64098-025-9 • ISBN-10: 1-64098-025-3 (PDF ebook)

1. The Somerton Man (1905? - 1948). 2. The Somerton Man Case. 3. The Tamám Shud Case. 4. The Somerton Man Code. 5. Omar Khayyam (AD 1021-1123). 6. The Rubaiyat (Robaiyat) of Omar Khayyam. 7. Edward FitzGerald (1809-1881). 8. OKCIR: Omar Khayyam Center for Integrative Research. I. Mohammad H. Tamdgidi 1959- . II. Title.

First Edition: October 1, 2021
Front cover: "Russia. The Republic of Dagestan. Makhachkala, Dagestan State Philharmonic. Bas-Relief. A Man Dances Lezginka " (Dreamstime: 200909927) • The Somerton Man Autopsy Photo • The Somerton Man Code (also on Jacket flaps)
Back cover : "Bas-relief depicting a Couple Dancing the Folk Dance Lezginka, Makhachkala, Republic of Dagestan, Dagestan State Philharmonic, Bas-Relief" (Dreamstime: 20090177)
Front cover: Statue of Omar Khayyam, by Abolhasan Seddiqi, Laleh Park, Tehran, Iran (by author)
Cover and Text Design: Ahead Publishing House, Belmont, MA, USA

The paper used in the print editions of this book is of archival quality and meets the minimum requirements of ANSI/NISO Z39.48-1992 (R1997) (Permanence of Paper). The production of this book on demand protects the environment by printing only the number of copies that are purchased.

for

The Somerton Man and Woman
who wished their last dance in love to last forever

Contents

Preface

In this OKCIR Research Report, hermeneutic sociologist, Khayyami scholar, and founding director of Omar Khayyam Center for Integrative Research (OKCIR), Mohammad H. (Behrooz) Tamdgidi, Ph.D., reports having solved the mystery of the code associated with the so-called "Somerton Man" or "Tamám Shud" case.

Given that the basic facts of the case have by now become widely known and are readily available online, and given the new findings about the code can shed radically new light on the details of what transpired, in what follows we will directly start with the code and its deciphering in detail after a basic brief introduction. Having learned what the code means, we will then come back to the wider story and interpret the details in light of the knowledge gained from deciphering the code.

Therefore, readers who have become more or less familiar with the case and have developed an opinion about The Somerton Man (TSM) and what transpired in 1948 (and thereafter) are encouraged to temporarily suspend their views and judgments to date about the case, so that they can consider the code's meaning before reconsidering their perspectives.

The reason is that, as the findings to be reported will also demonstrate, we as observers are not really separate from what we observe and the conclusions we reach from such observations, since our views and opinions have influenced and will continue to influence our understanding of the case. Therefore, being self-reflective about rethinking our prior views of the Somerton Man case is itself a requirement of the code's deciphering and can itself contribute to understanding what transpired in this sad but interesting story—one that can also offer us new insights about how we can and should go about solving long-standing puzzles in human life.

For the purpose of illustration and confirmation of meanings in this decoding, online resources will be used, with live links in the digital editions of this research report. Given the dynamic nature of online addresses, it is possible that following the publication of this report one or another address may change. However, by noting the main home addresses of the links, readers can trace the site tools used for deciphering purposes by reentering the intended words again. If any questions arise regarding changed linkages, please contact OKCIR for further updates. Moreover, to avoid crowding the report's basic text flow in the printed editions of this research report, reference linkages are offered not in the text itself or as footnotes, but will be shared as endnotes.

This report is comprised only of basic text with reference links, without any images inside beside the Somerton Man's code since all the images relevant to the case can be found widely online. The printed editions of this report (in softcover or hardcover) are also available in digital format for book readers (EPub and PDF). They can be ordered from most online bookstores and also from the Okcir Bookstore.

Disclaimer: This research report is published for informational purposes, and contains findings about an historical event and a person's suicide in the past and matters pertaining to his life and death. The study is investigative and explorative, not prescriptive in any way, shape, or form. It is an effort in understanding the circumstances surrounding an event and the nature of what transpired, which include understanding hermeneutically the mind-set and perspectives held by the person or persons related to the matter of suicide. Therefore, the findings should in no way be considered as an advocacy for any decision resulting in suicide and ending human life. Life is the most precious gift anyone can receive and enjoy. If you or someone you know struggles with issues pertaining to mental and physical health or self-harm, you should directly and immediately consult a medical professional or mental health consultant in your local or wider community in the nation in which you live.

1. Introduction: The Somerton Man Case

The Somerton Man (TSM) or 'Tamám Shud' case has over the past seven decades gained such global fame, raised so much curiosity, attracted so much attention, and been so widely reported, archived, and documented in the media, that it hardly needs an introduction.

It suffices here to say that on December 1, 1948, an unknown man was found dead neatly dressed up and lying down on the ground with legs crossed on The Somerton Park beach, located south of Adelaide in South Australia, Australia, without any specific personal identifications on him.

Among what was found on and eventually from him (aside from a suitcase of belongings he had left in a train station before his death, with some cloth markings removed as was the case for those he was wearing) was a small scrap of paper rolled and deeply hidden in the fob pocket of his pants on which was printed 'Tamám Shud' (a transliteration of two Persian words that together mean "it's finished," "it ended," or "it's done").

The piece was later found to have been torn from the last page of a first edition copy of Edward FitzGerald's free translations of Omar Khayyam's *Rubaiyat*. The small book from which the 'Tamám Shud' piece was torn was itself found later by someone in his car and handed in to the investigators. The booklet had been apparently tossed in from an open window of the car sometime before TSM died.

The details of the case are vast and the basics can be found on the Wikipedia page for the Somerton Man case also known as the "Tamám Shud case" here[1]. Nowadays endless blogs and audiovisual material (such as those on YouTube) can be found online by searching for the case (for example see the first of the Somerton Case lecture series here[2], with another section and other clips and interviews also available). Extensive archival materials and interviews about, and documentary and news coverage of, the case have also been made available widely online (see for instance here[3] and the resources gathered here[4]). Books and other reports have also been published on the subject, such as the example here[5].

Clearly, any new findings about TSM, such as those being shared in this report, owes much to decades of efforts made by various investigators, authors, experts, academics, and those in the broader public, who have spent much time to solving the puzzle.

The interest about the case has been so enduring that recently, following continued failures to identify TSM, his body was exhumed on May 19, 2021, for deeper DNA analysis (for further news and information see for example here[6] or here[7]). The DNA analysis investigation is still underway at the time of publication of this report, aiming to find answers that can shed final light on the identity and the story of the deceased man.

By way of his research center named after Omar Khayyam, the transdisciplinary and transcultural sociologist Mohammad H. Tamdgidi has since 2002 dedicated time to understanding and helping solve social problems. In recent years he has focused on unriddling high-profile enigmas in science and Khayyami studies whose reports have been published and are still in progress. Until recently, he had not paid much attention to the Somerton Man case. However, following the recent official exhumation of TSM's body in May 2021 and given the associations of the case with Omar Khayyam and his poetry and the renewed official and personal efforts made by many over the decades to exhume the deceased's body to identify him in order to bring closure and peace to those who may be his new or old relatives, Dr. Tamdgidi decided to devote some time to help with solving the case by way of deciphering the coded message found on the copy of the *Rubaiyat* edition associated with TSM.

Following an initially unsuccessful attempt at deciphering the code by considering any interest TSM may have had in mapping the differences between the various editions of Edward FitzGerald's translation with one another, Tamdgidi recently succeeded in discovering the key to deciphering the code. Even then, however, it required successive efforts at interpreting the words TSM had left behind. The final details of the findings are now being shared in this research report.

Although important insights can be gained into TSM's identity in light of the findings reported here, the focus of this effort is mainly on the code itself, explaining how it was deciphered and what it means. The Somerton Man case is much wider and more complex than the code itself, of course, and the purpose here is not to delve too deeply into the wider aspects of the story beyond possible hints the code's deciphering can offer to all those interested regarding the identity of the person and the nature of the events surrounding his death.

Given what the code's deciphering can reveal about the possible geographical roots of TSM's ancestry or even his possible surname or nickname, Tamdgidi hopes that the new information will help narrow down and focus the efforts underway by specialists in analyzing his DNA and physical remains in favor of bringing a closure to this case. There is still much to be learned and discovered about TSM, so this report can hopefully be another new beginning toward resting the case in a fruitful way.

2. The Code: Preliminary Observations

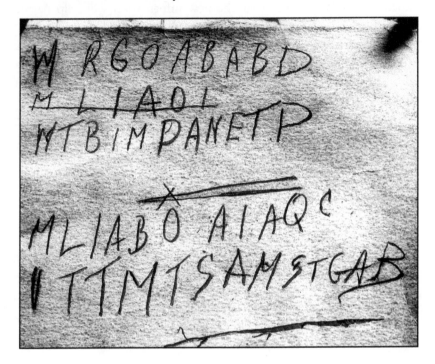

As it can be seen in the above image, the so-called 'code' is comprised of four main lines of capitalized letters (apparently including no numbers), with an additional line of capitalized letters crossed out (or, very unlikely, underlined) between the first and the second main lines of the code. The crossed-out line letters seem to be incorporated back into the third main line of the code with some changes. In what follows, the code will be considered to have four main lines, plus a crossed-out line between the first and the second main lines, not counted as part of the four main lines of the code.

The code also contains a horizontal set of double lines before the third main line of the code, extending over the top of some letters of the third main line with a cross (x) appearing on the double-line over the letter O. Another single line is also drawn on the bottom of the code as a whole, as if signifying the end of the code.

It is important to keep in mind in what follows that the code letters

P, but decided after his first try that the circle of P is too small and that he should also capitalize it like other letters of the code, so he traced a larger curve for the P such that it instead ended up appearing much larger than usually rendered for the letter. Perhaps, due to not being native in English, he may have thought that is the way to make the p capitalized as a P in English. For this reason, the smaller M preceding the large-curve P can be considered compatible in terms of size, since TSM must have finished writing the M before the P, when he realized the P should be "capitalized" more prominently than he had first tried.

Overall, the above observations may be considered in favor of the notion that TSM was not native in English writing—hinting at his migrant background. This does not mean he could not read or write in English at all, since obviously he was reading Khayyam in FitzGerald's English translation. Besides, the *Rubaiyat* translation can also offer an interesting textbook for learning English. One can be multilingual without necessarily being native in English language.

Also, as will be explained in the decoding solution key offered later below, it is more likely that the two ambiguous Ws at the beginning of the main lines 1 and 2 are Ws, not Ms. That is because, first, other Ms are clearly rendered consistently in the code as Ms, so there is less reason to believe the ambiguous letters are Ms. Second, W by itself (with or without a space between it and a following word) can have a meaning in the code's language environment as it will be explained (such as standing for "and" or "with" or "while" as we shall explain) but M alone by itself does not have a meaning.

Once we establish independently from these letters that the code is indeed rendered in a transliteration environment from another language, then the above ambiguities can be more fruitfully clarified and understood. Again, we should always keep in mind that the ambiguity of those two W letters may have also been originally due to TSM's own effort in trying to find a way of transliterating an expression he had in mind, so as he was sketching his draft code, he may have changed his mind, going over the letter again trying to decide how to express his mind and/or feelings.

The code image also displays a set of double lines over the "BO AIAQC" with an "x" over the O and on the double lines. One of the double lines (at least) may have extended in part on the right to the C and beyond it in the original fainter tracing before the code was rendered in darker lines by the police agent during investigation, as it is still noticeable on the right upon zooming on the image; but accepting that consideration is not vital to deciphering the code. Later below, the double-line's significance in the overall code will be explained.

There is also a single line on the bottom of the whole code, which indicates TSM meant the writing of what he intended to write to have been completed above that line.

3. Preliminary Interpretive Considerations

An important interpretive consideration in deciphering this code is the following.

If we decipher the code to be a poem, such as ones Khayyam composed and were freely translated by FitzGerald, we should keep in mind that a text can have multiple meanings, especially in the context of a poem, and that it can also be translated differently by others.

Therefore, even if we had a text or poem clearly written down rather than mysteriously coded, we could still wonder about its many meanings, and the many meanings themselves can be intentional depending on the skills and the depth of imagination of its author. To this day, many still wonder what Khayyam meant by this or that word, this or that trope or metaphor, in his poems. So, it should not surprise us if differences of opinion arise on the meaning of the code, even when its words have been decoded.

However, it will be shown below that despite such possible intended (or not) alternative meanings, we can clearly arrive at a sense of what the code is about in its overall meaning and what other possible meanings could be, all still contributing to the understanding of what TSM meant to convey through his code.

A further interpretive consideration to be given is that the code was written in the year 1948, more than seven decades ago, in the shadow of WWII, in circumstances involving multilingual and transcultural modes of communication, plus involving code writing skills of someone who knew but may not have been native in English, having also been possibly involved in intelligence communications to some extent.

So, the choice of words, and the forms and expressions of the letters as used in the code must be taken into such contextual considerations. If TSM had been involved in a spying career and practiced code-writing while taking advantage of his multilingual skills, deciding to write his poem in an uncommon style to engender mystery and enigma would be a plausible consideration, even though the code itself had little to do with military or intelligence matters.

4. Using Online Resources to Illustrate the Decoding

In what follows, Google Translate[8] (GT) and other dictionaries or online resources will be used to explain, illustrate, or support various findings. GT is not perfect, though is improving by day, and its quality varies from language to language and direction of translation, but at times it can also helpfully illustrate the various approximate meanings for the words being translated.

Note that the meaning of a word alone in GT can change when used as part of a multiple-word line. TSM's code is not necessarily meant to be a completely constructed and grammatically complete statement, but uses words as hint words to express meanings in association with others on the same line and in relation to other lines of the code as a whole. So, we should generally treat the words as individual words in GT for best results, while considering also what they could mean on the lines in which they appear, keeping in mind that even the line-reading of multiple words in GT are not necessarily perfect.

Another consideration regarding GT is that depending on diacritics added for a language, the meaning of a word can also change. But, if the code does not as a rule use letters to denote unwritten diacritics, which is the case with TSM's code as it will be shown, we are on a firm ground in unambiguously mapping the code's main letter structure in the language it is constructed. Some of the intended words are so obvious when transliterated that for those native in the language it is readily clear what the word means. For others, further explanation may be needed to interpret the text, but once explained they also prove to be clear in their meaning amid the code as a whole.

GT also gives, helpfully, a working non-standard transliteration of non-English letters when translating them, also offering pronunciations using the speaker icon. This can be seen below the text in the box on the left of the GT page (along with the pronunciation icon). While the GT transliteration is not to be confused with TSM's transliteration, since the GT transliteration includes the diacritics, for the non-native readers GT's transliteration can be helpful in ascertaining the interpretation being made. Often times, once the diacritic-representing letters are removed from the GT transliteration, the resemblance of it to that offered by TSM becomes evident.

5. 'Tamám Shud' Is Also the Decoding Key

As it is well-known, what led investigators to the poetry booklet was a small piece of paper torn out from the end of a first edition copy of Edward FitzGerald's free translation of Omar Khayyam's poetry titled *The Rubaiyat of Omar Khayyam*, where FitzGerald transliterated the Persian expression تمام شد using English letters as 'Tamám Shud.'

The expression means in Persian "it ended," "it's done," "it's finished," or "it's completed"; in Persian, the expression "Tamám Shud" or "Tamám Kard" can also connote someone having died. So, dying is also one of the connotations of the word, even though FitzGerald did not mean it that way in the context in which he used it. FitzGerald basically intended to mark the end of his translation after the last quatrain of the collection by offering that transliterated expression from Persian. He simply meant to say, his translation of the quatrains was finished. He was basically saying the common expression "The End" using a transliteration from the Persian expression of the word.

TSM was observant of how a Persian expression ('Tamám Shud') was transliterated into English letters for a non-Persian speaking audience. And this would have been even more significant for him as a style of coded communication, if he was himself familiar at least with the Arabic letters used also in Persian language. His putting the torn-out piece into his fob pocket can therefore be regarded as an important gesture or signal on TSM's part in offering a "key" to deciphering any code he may have left, if he intended such a use as a "bread crumb," so to speak, for deciphering his code.

Given that he had the torn-out piece in his fob pocket and he had tossed its originating booklet in a car (rather than in trash, discarding it), indicates that TSM had hoped and considered it possible that, following his public suicide, those finding the booklet may share it with others, say the person whose phone number was also present on the booklet page and/or the investigators searching for his identity following his death.

But the following is a most important finding. The 'Tamám Shud' was not just a bread crumb to the code; it also offered *the key to deciphering it*. The key to deciphering the code is that it is also constructed using, like the expression 'Tamám Shud,' Arabic alphabet transliteration letters. However, unlike 'Tamám Shud' the meanings are expressed in Arabic language, not in Persian, nor in Turkish (although all these languages share many common words, a few of which are also found in the code). So, even the few Persian/Turkish shared words in the code are expressed in an Arabic language environment.

It is apparent that TSM was natively, or intimately by training or education, familiar with the Arabic language. This does not mean necessarily that he was ethnically Arab or from an Arabic speaking community, though he could have been one way or another. After all, FitzGerald used Persian transliteration for 'Tamám Shud' without that implying he was Persian. TSM could have had a multilingual background and training while not being Arab ethnically *per se*, though the latter we may not be able to easily rule out when other clues in what he left behind can also be taken into consideration. It just happens that TSM, being intimately familiar with Arabic for one or another reason, decided to creatively render his poetic code or note also in the 'Tamám Shud' style.

TSM's 'code' is basically a transliteration, as if trying to follow the example of 'Tamám Shud' style (a general table of transliteration or Romanization from Arabic can be found here[9]). His code's Arabic is not necessarily that used in major Arab nations, however, since he may have been familiar with a local Arabic dialect prevalent in specific communities, say, in the Caucasus regions at the time in the Soviet Union (or Russia today). For example, the Arabic he was familiar with could have been Shirvani Arabic, which was once spoken in the Azerbaijani and Dagestani regions of the Caucasus (see here[10]).

The above will be further explained below, but we should note again the historical time-frame and context in which TSM lived. If he was born around 1905 in, say, the Caucasus, he would have been born in pre-Soviet Russia, where communities in the region still spoke a local Arabic dialect using traditional Arabic alphabet, meaning that TSM could have grown up knowing Arabic, while also speaking Russian (and other languages and dialects, such as Azeri and Turkish using Arabic alphabet before both began later on using Cyrillic or Latin alphabets respectively).

It is important to keep in mind that cultures in the broader Middle Eastern and Caucasus regions are deeply cross-cultural in language, so you can easily find Persian and Turkish words even in their Arabic communications. We should not forget that a great part of the region was under Persian, Arab, or Ottoman, rule for centuries, so it is possible that in a community you find folks using Turkish or Persian amid communications in Arabic, the reverse of this being also true.

In Iran for instance the population is multi-ethnic including Persians, Arabs, Kurds, Azeris, Lors, Baluchis, Turkmans, and so on, some extending deeply into the Caucasus. So, in the languages of the region Persian, Arabic, Turkish, and other words and names can be co-present. For the same reason, speaking Arabic should not automatically imply being religiously Muslim. In Lebanon, for instance, you have Arabs who are Muslim (of various sects), Christian, Druze, Armenian, Jewish, or atheist socialists. This is even more the case for the deeply and widely multi-ethnic population in the Caucasus.

However, despite such multilingual varieties, we will find that TSM's code is expressed clearly and consistently using transliterated letters from Arabic. The text gives the impression of having been written as a secretive code, rather than being a straightforward text with separated words, but it was not necessarily intended as such to conceal any military or intelligence information or anything similar. It is just an effort to write and leave a transliterated note in 'Tamám Shud' style, being inspired by that notion, making it hard to decipher for one reason or another, especially if the intention was deliberately to embroil events in deep, lasting mystery. But once it is known and deciphered to be constructed as an Arabic transliteration, its meaning becomes rather clear and obvious. TSM was trying to be creative with the style of his note, which may itself be telling of his having had an artistic, literary, creative spirit or inclination, being even involved in performing arts for example, given his physical features telling of someone seriously trained in the dancing arts.

As it will be explained, there are two non-Arabic words by exception in the code (MPANETP and AIAQC). But their exceptions in fact will be shown to prove the rule, that is, the Arabic transliteration key for deciphering the code. In other words, their renderings show that Arabic transliteration and expression rules of the code are applied consistently since one of them, MPANETP, including twice the letter P not found in Arabic alphabet (as can be seen in the standard transliteration table for Arabic found here[11], shared earlier), must be part of a medical illness name abbreviation (MPAN or MPAN ETP, if we choose to read the last letter of that line as a P) using English letters. If the last letter of the second main line is regarded as D, ETD can also be unambiguously interpreted as an Arabic word without undermining the overall meaning of the code.

The second exception word is that of the rendering of an originally Turkish word AIAQC that appears in various spellings and renditions even today in Persian and Arabic, and more specifically across the Caucasus region (such as in Dagestan, a region that was a part of the Soviet Union, and is still now an autonomous republic in Russia) from where TSM may have ethnically come from himself or by way of his ancestral parentage (beside being broadly Russian), even though he may have lived and/or visited elsewhere in the world before visiting Adelaide for the last time.

The last letter of that word, an accented C, is what is often rendered as C' or Ç, sounding like "ch" as in "church." This letter also does not exist in standard Arabic alphabet, and its use by TSM indicates that the word, at least in one of its "double" or "multiple" meanings, is meant also as a proper or nickname, borrowed from another language. This important word will be explained later in this report.

Following WWII a new "fourth wave" of migrations to Australia from the broader Russian regions took place, and those arriving, even though they were ethnically different from being specifically Russian, still identified themselves as broadly Russian. So, they could speak fluently Russian while speaking also their own ethnic mother tongues as prevalent in their local land of origin in Russia (at the time Soviet Union). Further information about this can be read here[12] and here[13].

6. The Language Environment of the Code

Persian uses Arabic alphabet, plus the additional letters p as in Peter, zh as in Zhivago, g as in Good, and ch as in Chair, letters that are generally absent in Arabic alphabet. However, it is important to note that there are languages (like Persian) using Arabic alphabet (even in Arabic context used in other communities in the region) that include some of those missing letters above. For example, Turkish which used to use Arabic alphabet, uses the letter ç for "ch". Or, in the alphabet for the language Dargwa of the Dagestan Autonomous Republic there is the letter ҫ which is transliterated as letter C with an accent, as can be seen here[14]. In fact, the capital city of Dagestan includes in its name Makhachkala "ch" or ç as a letter. That alphabet includes, like Persian, letters ژ and گ and چ plus other alphabet variations not found in Arabic. This does not mean the TSM code's language is Dargwa. It is the standard Arabic. But, for someone from any other community using Arabic alphabet, the additional letters can be known especially if the letters are used in proper names.

In Arabic and Persian some vowels and most diacritics are not written as stand-alone letters but appear as symbols above or below letters, often omitted in informal writing. So, someone who knows the language usually knows how to pronounce them in informal language; but in formal language, such as in religious texts, the use of diacritics is followed. In Arabic particularly, but even in Persian or other languages using Arabic, what diacritics are used where can change the meaning of a word.

The basic letters of The Somerton Man's code, however, can be unambiguously derived from a transliteration of them, because he consistently does *not* use letters for unwritten diacritics. The question of how his letters can be read and what meaning the word can acquire by adding diacritics would then be a separate matter, such that even if the code was literally written in Arabic, some may still ask what the word could mean or how it could be differently read. For example the word دم in Persian can be read as "dam" (دَم) meaning either breath or moment, or "dom" (دُم) for tail, the two meanings having little connection to one another in this case. If someone transliterated it without diacritics as "dm" one could still wonder if the author meant to say "dam" or "dom." But the fact that the letters "dm" are the actual written letters of the word is unambiguously rendered and the alternative readings of it can be posed whether it is written in its original alphabet or in transliteration.

A skilled poet may even play around with the different meanings or expressions of the same word to convey a message. Khayyam's poetry itself offers examples of such uses, where, say the word "bād" (wind) and "bādeh" (wine), or "dam" meaning at once "breath" and "moment," can be played with another, and still people debate to this day what he meant by "wine." In a quatrain, for example, Khayyam sarcastically played with the Persian word for wine, "sharāb," which is literally a coupling of the words "shar" and "āb" meaning respectively "bad (or evil)" and "water." So, in the poem, he is amused wondering why people refer to such a splendid Drink as "wine" (by which he actually may not even have the literal "wine" in mind, we must note, depending on the depth of our reading of his poetry and philosophy) "bad water." In other words, in the hands of a skilled poet, the same word can be thought as split into parts, or two separate words joined, to produce a variety of meanings.

In any case, if the diacritics are not included in the Arabic transliteration, the writing without them can appear as a series of consonant letters, which may seem odd and unusual for Western readers (such as ITTMT), leading them to think that they are meaningless letters coming after one another, not forming any words or sentences. So, such readers may be inclined to think instead that the letters do not make up words together, but each letter represents perhaps another word, and so on. But, such interpretive approaches can lead nowhere (and it has not, for decades), since there is no way one can know what different appearances of the same letter—say the many appearances of A or B or T, and so on—signify in representing other words, short of being given a key, leading to wild speculations about infinite possibilities for the code's meaning. That is why efforts at deciphering the code as a group of letters each representing a word has persistently failed.

If TSM was an intelligence worker or spy and familiar with code-writing using other languages, one way he could complicate things for others is by joining separate words to one another, or by splitting words that are supposed to be parts of the same word. This does not mean that the code he wrote was an intelligence or military secret, however. TSM could have had personal reasons to make the code less easily decipherable, such as trying to bolster the mysterious choreography of his own passing.

So, he may have used his intelligence code-writing skills and his personally rich multilingual background to convey a personal message, without the code itself hiding any military secrets.

To rule out Turkish as the code's language calls for further explanation. Turkish language (which by 1948 had already begun switching from using Arabic alphabet to Latin letters) directly uses transliterated letters in its writing to represent what used to be in its Arabic alphabet in the past. So, had TSM meant to use Turkish as a language environment for his code, we would find letters representing diacritics in the words' makeup, but we do not find them. If a vowel is found in the code (such as "A" it is because that vowel is itself represented as a stand alone letter in Arabic language).

TSM's code is consistently lacking *unwritten* diacritics in general. Even though some of the Arabic words of the code can also be understood in Persian and Turkish, the nature of the words as transliterated clearly suggests that the language environment of the code was intended to be Arabic. Whether the choice of the language was inevitable because TSM was ethnically Arab or of a culture using Arabic alphabet, or he chose to write the code in Arabic due to being multilingual or somehow professionally trained to do so (say as a code writer intimately familiar with Arabic as a coding language), is something to be considered further. In WWII, for instance, we know how U.S. military intelligence used Native American "code talkers" to communicate secret messages (see here[15]).

But, we can definitely rule out Turkish as being the lingual environment of the code and in fact that makes writing and reading the code more consistent and predictable. Those who have ruled out Persian or Arabic as being the language of the code because of the problem of diacritic renderings, should consider that the code in fact is NOT intended to include diacritics, but only the basic written letters. So, how a word such as, say, ملى , is to be interpreted can even be a challenge if the word was expressed using Arabic alphabet. For example, while that word in Persian can mean "national," in Arabic as ملﺀ it can also mean "for a long time" or "fill" depending on the diacritics used in context (citations for which will be given later in this report).

In the case of the code, it will be rather clear what the intended meaning is once it is deciphered, but the above should be kept in mind in the effort being made to reveal its meaning.

7. Strategies for Making the Code Difficult to Decipher

Given what is being reported in the code's content (as we shall see), involving matters of life and death and responsibility for terminating a life, even as an assisted suicide possibly involving the mother of TSM's son who was to take care of and raise the child, there is clearly an effort in making it not easily decipherable, unless provided the key. For example, had Jessica Thomson been accused of murdering TSM, she could have provided clues to how the code's writing could be deciphered, if necessary. But short of that, there would be no need for doing so.

The strategies used for making the code not easily decipherable can include the following: 1-Using a transliteration strategy from an unfamiliar (to one's intended audience) language and alphabet to convey the message, rather than writing a straightforward note or code in English; 2-The words of the code can be arbitrarily separated from one another or arbitrarily joined, which requires some effort to identify the words; 3-The code can be a group of individual hint words rather than complete sentences, serving simply to offer hints at meanings, rather than pretending to be composed of grammatically structured lines or paragraphs; 4-The language used to transliterate itself could have been a choice, both in terms of its being a non-Western language, and a specific language, that allows for not including diacritics as part of the words' makeup.

A series of consonant letters as such could be quite hard to crack and can lead many astray, which apparently has over the decades. If TSM had included the Arabic article "al-" anyone basically familiar with the language would have realized what the code's language is. If he had used a Turkish transliteration system, which includes the diacritics, readers familiar with the language would have more readily realized what the words are. Instead, in an Arabic transliteration environment lacking the diacritics, the row of consonant letters can seem like a random combinations of letters that would be harder to crack.

Transliteration from Arabic not including diacritics is a common practice, even though the words look odd as a series of consonant letters. In this[16] site offering an Arabic transliteration tool, for example, if you copy and paste محمد (for Mohammad), you will find it transliterated oddly as "mhmd". Or, if you paste تمام شد (for 'Tamám Shud') which is a Persian phrase but one that still uses Arabic letters, you will find it transliterated as "tmam shd" not 'Tamám Shud'; the reason "a" is still included in "tmam" is that the vowel is itself a stand-alone letter in the alphabet. So, even though it seems odd, The Somerton Man was not doing anything odd by transliterating from Arabic as he did in his code, with the text looking in parts like a series of consonant letters one after the other.

But, again, once the key to the decoding is revealed to be the Arabic language of the code, the text becomes clear in its lettering architecture, even though, as noted before, readers can still debate what the various alternative meanings of the words or lines in the code could be, or how best to translate them in meaning and in poetic style.

TSM most likely chose to transliterate from his own (presumably native or professionally trained in) language Arabic, being inspired by the example of 'Tamám Shud,' i.e., to write his final note—keeping in mind that Arabic is spoken in a variety of national and communal settings in the region. Still, realizing that those around him do not read Arabic, he just transliterated it instead, being inspired by the example of FitzGerald's note at the end of *The Rubaiyat*. Again, we do not have to immediately jump into the conclusion that simply because the code uses Arabic as its interpretive environment its author must be Arab ethnically. FitzGerald transliterated from Persian without being a Persian, so could TSM. Had FitzGerald chosen to do so, he could have rendered a Persian quatrain of Khayyam entirely in transliteration as he did with 'Tamám Shud' without being either an Arab or a Persian, since he had already become familiar with the Persian/Arabic alphabet. However, if other clues in TSM's life and end of life story suggest that indeed he knew Arabic natively as one of the languages he grew up with, and therefore he was in part Arab, ethnically or culturally, then, that is a different story we should consider.

Note that FitzGerald, when transliterating from the Persian تمام شد , included some unwritten vowels (diacritics) as part of his transliteration, which is how Persian is transliterated today as well (which also explains, by the way, why TSM's code is not a transliteration from Persian either). Had FitzGerald written it without the diacritics, it would have been something like "Tmam Shd" as noted previously. With diacritics تمام شد would be تَمَام شُد . So, the reason for his transliteration as such was that the first T has an unwritten diacritic following it in Persian (which would be Ta, as in Tag), and the same for the letter Sh, which would be "Shu" (actually, it should be more correctly pronounced in Persian as "Shod" which is also why رباعیات has been transliterated as Rubaiyat rather than, as more correctly pronounced in Persian, Robaiyat). Notice that the Alef ("a") (here sounding like that in All—usually transliterated with an accent, as á in 'Tamám Shud,' which FitzGerald actually used—is included in the transliteration because it is a lettered vowel that is supposed to sound like the 'a' in "Arm." TSM actually follows this rule consistently in the code, where "A" for Alef or ا is always included in the lettering.

8. Starting with the Last Main Line of the Code

Although, in order to read the code normally, we should obviously begin from its first line, since the lines of the code have their own meanings to express and the last line happens to be the least controversial and most representative of what the code is all about, let us begin with the last line as our decoding procedure.

The most interesting and revealing fourth and last main line of the code, one that even without the rest of the code nearly explains the whole story of what transpired in 1948, is comprised of five words: IT TMT SAM ST GAB

- The first two words IT TMT going together (as do 'Tamám Shud') stand for إت تمّ which mean "It's done," "It's completed," "It's finished," or "It's ended." This is basically an Arabic rendition for 'Tamám Shud,' meaning "It's done." تمّ (TMT) or done also has a connotation of dying (that is where the words "mate" or "checkmate" in chess come from, by the way, as if saying you're "dead," or the king's "dead").
- For the two words IT TMT rendered separately, GT offers the meaning "It's done" here[17]. In GT the meaning of the two words when connected is "she completed" as in here[18], so when the two are connected GT recognizes the gender reference. It is regarded as female referent because of the ا at the beginning of إت since Arabic conjugation is gendered. TSM uses an "I" to begin the word, not an Alef (he could have used an A instead of I but used the latter knowingly). The hamzeh usually stands for a small "i" when it comes at the beginning of a word, so it is proper to render that first letter as an "I" in transliteration, which can also mean that he was intentionally trying to imply a female referent.
- The word تمّ (TMT) is from the same root that the word "Tamám" comes from, actually, as in *The Rubaiyat* signature added by FitzGerald. Here, TSM is creatively playing with the pun on 'Tamám Shud,' and saying, in Arabic, "It's done" also implying "she completed," with the connotation of its being finished by a female referent. So, in Arabic he could say just "it's done" while conveying the gender aspect implicitly.
- As mentioned early in this report, note that GT has transliterated

on the lower left corner of the box the word here[19] almost like that of TSM's, once the diacritics are removed from the GT version (for example 'iittamat' or 'iit tamat,' when you take out the letters standing for the diacritics, becomes 'ittmt' or 'it tmt').

- Regarding the gender aspect, as we shall see, there is another word in the line that clearly conveys the female reference as well. So, there is a strong hint in the last line of the code at a female referent. In Arabic, words can be gendered (which is not the case in Persian).

- Let us not yet jump into conclusions regarding whether the female referent ended up actually being involved in "ending" whatever it was to end. The code could be simply a contemplated plan of intended action rather than a report of what actually happened. So, for now let us limit our effort to understanding the code on its own, than being yet concerned with its implications for the wider story.

- The second word SAM stands for سامّ or سَمّ which means "poisonous" or "poison" (in Arabic and Persian respectively). See GT here[20] for the illustration of this transliterated word in both versions. GT offers SAM for سام because it can also be a person's name, but if you double-click on the word سام in the GT linked page above you will see all the meanings in Arabic for the word relating to poison listed.

- The fact that the letter "A" is added in between S and M in TSM's code makes it even more apparent that the word is being expressed in Arabic, since in Persian the A is not used and instead it is rendered as a diacritic as in سَمّ (as in the two options previously linked in GT, again given here[21]).

- There is a repetition accent "shadda" (or in Persian "tashdid") on the letter M for SAM usually in both Arabic and Persian that is often omitted and not written. However, the word is always written with just one M, not two, as it is also rendered that way correctly by TSM in the code.

- Actually, given all the puzzles generated around how TSM died, it turns out ironically that the evidence for the use of poison, that is, the word سامّ or سَمّ was right in front of us in the code all these decades in almost the biggest letters of the code!

- The GT transliteration SAM for سام here[22] which is what TSM intends to say is verbatim as given by TSM. The code of course does not go into details of whether the poison was to be ingested or injected (or inhaled, even though the investigations suggested smoking items were not poisonous; perhaps TSM could have smoked the poison discarding the cigarettes elsewhere or deeper under the sands). Poetically speaking, even "drinking a cup of poison" could stand for being poisoned, no matter by what method. Also, again, let us keep in mind that the code, being written by TSM is obviously projecting an action into the future, rather than something already done.

- The next word ST can be read either connected or not to its next word GAB. But for now, considered alone, it has the primary meaning of the number 6 or six. It is unlikely that TSM meant by the word the number 6, as if pointing to a six-ingredient poison. Remotely it could refer to the time taken, but why go into such detail in such a short note?

- It is most likely that TSM used ST in its second meaning which is سيّده in Arabic, which means "lady," as can be seen in the option 2 given by GT here[23]. In Arabic-English dictionary the two meanings of the word can be found here[24] for سِت . In context, TSM must have the latter in mind, and as such makes it clear again that he is specifically addressing a female in this last line of the code. Basically by سِت TSM is referring to a female referent as a "lady."

- GAB which stands for غاب means "missed" or "absent." But, we should be careful not to interpret the word primarily as being related to the meaning "missing someone" (even though as a possibility in a poetic context, that could also be a secondary possibility, since when we say we miss someone, we are literally implying they are absent for us).

- The word GAB is translated by GT here[25] as "missed" to be primarily interpreted in terms of making oneself absent, of vanishing, of hiding oneself from the public, keeping a low profile, keeping distance. Basically, it means "evade." If the word

GAB is connected to the word سـت before it as in سـتغاب GT offers the approximate meaning "you will be missed" here[26]. However, it would be misleading to interpret that primarily in terms of "missing someone" *per se*, since what GT is really meaning in the translation is in terms of "be absent."

- In Arabic-English dictionary, the word غاب offers many related meanings that also include, "be hidden," "be masked," "fail to appear," "fail to attend," "be absent, be away," "be far from," "be distant from," "keep away from," "stay away from," "distance oneself from," as can be found here[27]. Again, these are different ways of saying "evade," or "be evasive." All these make it clear that TSM, being aware of its multiple meanings, uses the word غاب quite skillfully, and since it constitutes his last word of the code, he even renders it in a signature form as if finishing with style as a calligraphy.

- As those familiar with the Persian quatrain style in poetry know, the last line is always a punch line, where the shock of the poem is introduced. And here we have it from TSM. The last line is clearly a punch line as a whole, and the last word even an important 'punch word' on its own, so to speak. The word GAB in just one word can explain why we never found Jessica Thomson revealing the identity of TSM.

- Imagine someone using the word "be missed" in a message. It can mean "make yourself absent" but also "you will be missed" at once. A misunderstanding about texts especially in a poetic context is that they have to definitely mean A or B, and not both. Such an expectation arises from a formal logical thinking where simultaneity of meanings is not allowed, and is characteristic of Newtonian, chunky way of thinking using formal logic. Poetic language accommodates more readily quantum ways of thinking that allow for simultaneity and superposition of meaning. Any skilled poet using metaphors knows that in a single word many, sometimes even conflicting, meanings can be conveyed, and TSM seems to have been skilled in using poetic language in his final note intended for the mother of his child (her actually receiving it on Nov. 30, 1948, being a separate matter, we should keep in mind for now).

- Still, it is important to keep in mind that while the primary meaning of "evade" or "keep distance" is expressed, there is also a secondary hint at someone missing another person. After all, he seems to have been inspired by one of the most skilled poets of the world of all time, Omar Khayyam, who could condense literally hundreds of meanings in the space of four lines! Khayyam has been a caravan leader not only of mathematics and astronomy, but also of Persian poetry (along with Ferdowsi, who just preceded him). Hafez, Sadi, and Rumi came long after him. In any case, TSM's dominant intention here is to remind the lady to evade and keep distance, with a secondary implicit hint of missing her following the poisoning.

- The letter G is a transliteration for the letter غ in Arabic. In Persian, the letter غ is usually transliterated as "gh" and the reason is as follows. In Persian, as noted previously, there is a letter گ as in dog, for which G is used often in Persian transliteration. Arabic does not have that letter, however. So, using the letter "g" alone unambiguously transliterates to غ in Arabic. In Turkish just "g" is used for that letter, but it is used with an accent on top as in ğ . So, even without it, the letter unambiguously stands for غ in Arabic.

- The word GAB or غاب is related in Arabic (and Persian) to the word غايب or غيب or similar words most familiar to Arabic and Persian speakers, which connote being absent or unseen, implying to be missed, when someone is absent. As we shall see TSM is consistent with the transliteration use of the letter G for the Arabic letter غ in his code, as he uses the letter consistently on the first line of the code as well. TSM knew the basic protocols of his Arabic transliteration effort.

- The last line of the code and the words ST GAB or ست غاب in a way says it all in terms of this having been intended to be an assisted suicide note, since TSM is obviously expressing acceptance for such an ending to his life, and is acknowledging that there is another person involved in the plot who is supposed to be evasive and keep distance after the suicide. The event was not a case of murder, or something that implies TSM was not expecting such an ending to his life. But, again, we should keep in mind that the poem is projecting something into a future and not necessarily a report of an action done. Whether or not the "lady" referred to actually was present and participated in his last day's act, the code spoke of an imagined intention on the part of TSM regarding her as an aid in his suicide drama choreography, broadly speaking.

- The last line of the code overall is so telling and so significant hermeneutically that even if we let go of all the previous lines of the code, this last line alone makes it clear without any ambiguity what was intended to take place on that day in 1948, that it was meant to be a case of an assisted suicide, how it was imagined to be done, and who (a female) was intended to help him do it willingly on his part, even if her involvement was limited to only being a supportive mother of his child and being aware that the suicide was taking place. It was clearly NOT a criminal act against the will of TSM, but one in which he was more or less directly assisted by a female who was imagined to supply and/or administer a drug and/or at least be present when it was done to terminate his life by way of suicide, while it must have been (if also proven following the DNA tests) it was arranged that she raise their child.

- Our having started with the last and most definitively interpreted line has given us now a chance to confirm that the operating language of the code is indeed Arabic, and it is rendered in Arabic transliteration. So, we now proceed further to other lines of the code.

9. The Third Main Line of the Code

The third main line of the code is comprised of the following: MLI AB O AIAQC. Although in relation to this line we can also examine the crossed-out line comprised of MLIA OI or MLI AOI, for the time being let us focus on the third main line of the code by itself.

- The third main line has the added complication (beside the basic letters) of the double lines on some of the letters and the cross on the lines above the letter O. The double lines extend above the letters starting from B and seems to be ending on Q. However, it is unclear whether at least one of the two lines had originally extended further to the right over and beyond the C, since the upper line faintly continues further than the darkened part of the line, part of which is even still visible further to the right upon zooming. In other words, it may have been due to the darker tracing done later by the police agent that we do not have at least the upper of the double lines further extended on the right over and beyond the letter C.

- There can be a variety of explanations for the double lines, about which we cannot be absolutely certain, of course. However, some plausible interpretation of why the double lines exist will be provided further below.

- While it is unlikely, TSM may have been hinting that the letters below the double lines should be read as one piece, despite the existing space between the O and A. He may have decided that how he separated O from AIAQC is to be revised to be read as one piece without the space, so instead of crossing out and rewriting the whole line, he simply used the double lines to suggest that the letters below the lines are to read as one piece. However, given that TSM does not seem to be trying to be word-spacing correct, so to speak, in the code, and seems to be in fact using the word spacing feature as a complicating code-writing strategy, the effort to "correct" separated words with double lines would seem unnecessary and self-defeating. So, we should assume that TSM meant that the double lines indicate the expression below is to be regarded as one piece, without implying that the space between O and AIAQC is redundant. For example, if he intended to say,

"O boy," the double lines over both would suggest that he meant the expression as a whole, with O not to be used with prior letters to form words.

- The cross over O may alternatively have been meant to suggest that upon further consideration the double-lines should end on O and not extend to the left of it to B. If we compare this third main line of the code with the crossed-out line, of which it may be another rendition in part, a difference is the addition of the letter B between A and O on the crossed-out line. So, this may explain why TSM was trying to leave out the B from the meanings intended for the double lines. We cannot be sure, however, since this third main line of the code overall seems to be very prominent and not crossed out, so we can assume that the double lines starting with letter O and including AIAQC is to be read as a one-piece expression, having a central significance in the code. So, we may consider that the "x" would signify that TSM wants the expression at the end of the third line to start from O, and not before it.

- TSM may have also meant by the cross over the O to suggest that it should not be transliterated as a و but as an expression, such as found in "O sir," plenty of similar examples (as Lo! in quatrains 1, 7, 13, 21 or "Oh" in quatrains 12, 38, 57, 58) appearing in FitzGerald's translation of Khayyam's quatrains in the booklet. If TSM intended this code and this line to be a poem, he may have been trying to find a way of transliterating "O ... ." We can never be absolutely sure of this in the code, of course, but in the context of the rest of the line we may be able to find a plausible interpretation for the cross on the O, beside its serving to move the left edge of the double lines to O from B.

- Let us begin with the last part of the third main line of the code more or less under the double-lines, that is AIAQC. In Arabic transliteration context AIAQC can stand for ايا قیچ .

- Observers have wondered a lot about the appearance of the letters Q and also the smaller-looking accented "c" in the line, leading to many speculations about their meaning and significance. However, once we recognize the Arabic-transliteration nature of the code, both puzzles become clearly solved.

- Q stands for the letter ق in Arabic alphabet, which is used as such even today. TSM is consistent in his different notations for this letter Q for ق in contrast to the letter G for غ .

- The letter "c" which seems smaller and accented on top could be read in Arabic transliteration context as standing either for an ع (when written in very small type as in `) or also for the letter چ that appears in Persian, Turkish, and even in more specific dialects of Arabic as found, for example, in the Dagestan (of the Caucasus region of Russia) Arabic alphabet for the language Dargwa of the Dagestan Autonomous Republic as can be seen here[28]. In that system, the letter is written as Č. You can see that the accent for it is on top, rather than on the bottom, which can be hermeneutically significant in tracing the ethnic roots of TSM.

- If c as in ` stood for an accent standing for ع in Arabic, the word would be اياقع which is an unfamiliar and non-existing word in Arabic and GT confuses it sometimes as meaning "reality" as in here[29]. It is a very remote possibility and TSM himself may have preferred to use E as a transliteration for the letter ع in Arabic, which are somewhat similar in their curvatures and appearance (more on this later). The interpretation of the accented letter C' as چ , however, is significant and meaningful in the code, on which we will focus here.

- The letter "I" in AIAQC stands for ى which can also be rendered in transliteration as Y. The letter Q has also been transliterated as K (for example, the word Quran has also been transliterated as Koran), such that searching online it is common to find spellings such as Ayakçi for the same word in Turkish; the fact that TSM uses Q for it again points to his using Arabic language for writing the code, to his knowing his Arabic well, and to his having the Arabic spelling of the word in mind (with ق). In Ottoman Turkish, which used to use Arabic as alphabet, the word was rendered as اياقچى as can be seen here[30], and in modern Turkish using Latin alphabet, it is rendered as Ayakçi as can be seen here[31]. If you find a Persian speaker transliterate the word, you will find it done as Ayaqchi or Ayaghchi, for example, since in Persian the letter چ is transliterated as "ch" usually. In any case, all these variations are legitimate transliterations for اياقچى .

- The word اياقچى is pronounced by clicking on the speaker icon as found here[32], where it is spelled using Y for "I" and there is an I at the end. If you listen to the pronunciation you notice the "i" at the end is not noticeably pronounced. In contrast, it can also be pronounced like here[33], but does not have to be as such, so the "i" can be simply omitted in the transliteration; the dropping accent on C by TSM may have been actually intended to point to the tiny "I" sound at the end. If TSM was going to transliterate اياقچى it is fair to say just a C with accent at the end suffices. In Persian quatrain form, the third line does not have to rhyme with the first, second, and fourth lines. So, whether or not we read AIAQÇ as ending with an I or not, it does not challenge the quatrain form requirements of the code.

- In the Russian spelling of the word with the "I" at the end, you find an interesting search result here[34] referring in a newspaper of the Communist Party of Azerbaijan in Baku in 1958. The term here аиакчи is used in terms of "footworkers" implying "masses" (as in the grassroots), or in terms of "rising" or "awakening (masses)" since Ayak can also mean rising, standing up, or waking up, implying relation to feet, as will be explained below. In Turkish, if you say "dour ayaqa" it means "stand up" and "wake up" at once.

- The word اياقچى is a very important word with multiple meanings. First, even to this day, it is used as a proper name for people from the wider Caucasus region, such as Azerbaijan (even in Iran), Turkey, and presumably also from the Russian Caucasus such as Dagestan area as well. It is actually a word that appears also in historical manuscripts. Also, as اياقچى it appears in search results here[35] or searching for it as ayaqçi here[36] in Google search as names of people, in old documents, in cultures speaking Persian, Turkish, Kazakh (which refers to the same people known also as Cossacks), etc.

- The word "Ayaq" or "Aiaq" or "Ayak" means in Turkish "foot" as shown here (Ayak[37]), but it can also mean "cup," having

Turkish and Mongolian-Turkish roots (see the Persian dictionary result here[38]), perhaps because some wine cups used to have one or more "legs" under them (as in wine glasses used today).

- The word "Ayaqçi" (or in TSM "AIAQÇ" or "AIAQC'") also means "errand boy" or "footman" or "message boy" or "messenger boy" (here[39]) as someone who does the run around in trade, or even serving water, tea, or wine in ceremonies (see the Persian dictionary result here[40]). In Turkish for example it means "errand boy" as in here[41]. In Persian, it means the wine-server, or as اياغچى (see here[42]) or اياقچى here[43] as in Saqi or Saki as is known to those familiar with Persian poetry, as also found plentifully in Khayyam's quatrains. The word has a connotation of humbleness, of someone who does the footwork of serving others, but, in Sufism and esoteric Islam, its meaning can be as high as the Active Intellect, or what in Christianity is referred to as the Holy Spirit. The word آياق or اياغ appears in Ottoman Turkish dictionary combinations (see here[44]). So, if someone was evoking drinking a cup of poison from the hands of Saqi or Ayaqçi, it can also have a spiritual meaning as well.

- The word "Saqi" as wine-server used in Persian and Arabic (even appearing in FitzGerald's later 101 quatrains editions, not his 75 quatrains edition which TSM was using, as part of the last quatrain's first line "And when like her, oh, Saki, you shall pass") is basically another word for Ayaqçi, both meaning someone who runs around presumably on foot serving water, tea, or wine, like an errand boy. Saqi can also be female referent in Persian poetry.

- The word "Saqi" actually comes from "Saq" or ساق meaning "leg" (from the knee to the foot ankle) in Persian and Arabic, and explains why this word is used in Persian poetry for the one who goes around on foot and serves wine, be that a male or a female.

- Just as an example for its use as a proper name, a village in Iran's Kurdistan is named Ayaghchi (see here[45]), and another village is named Ayakchi in Uzbekistan (see ayakchi[46]). These are examples simply to show that the word, in various spellings and transliterations, is defused as a proper name for persons or places in the wider West Asian, Middle Eastern region.

- If you look for ancestry names, also, you will find a variety of renditions of basically the same name, such as "Ayakçi" (someone born in 1926 and dead in 1956), or a "Loi Is Aiakc" who died in Feb. 1948 (notice how the latter name does not have an 'I' at the end, almost as spelled by TSM, except for using K instead of Q, which is a common way such names are Romanized when the person moves to the West), or a "Geo Ayakse" born in 1889 in Russia, arriving in New York in 1921. These are just examples for how one can find proper names that seem to have same cultural roots. The above examples are offered without necessarily implying those persons have anything to do with TSM specifically, but only as instances of how the word can be used a proper name.

- The word AIAQC is so widely disseminated in the region's culture that it has been part of the vocabulary used in dancing arts, whether folklore, such as in Azeri or Caucasus dances (see here[47], for example, where an Iranian Azeri is explaining that the last dancer in a row of Azeri ancient Yalli folk dancers is called ayaqci or (اياقچی), or, even in a study of dance ceremonies related to Bektashi Sufi order in Turkey you find the word used (see here[48], searching in the document for ayakçı).

- The word AIAQC by itself could be a name, or a reference to someone whose career is similar to an "errand boy," "footman," or even a "spy" involved in running around passing messages. A spy could presumably call himself or herself or others doing similar work an Ayaqçi, and intelligence footworker. It can even be used metaphorically for a dancer, doing "footwork."

- However, in the context of the line of the code, AIAQC seems to be most prominently intended in its meaning as the wine-server, as in the Khayyami trope of the Saqi or Saki. TSM is basically trying to refer to the person helping him with assisted suicide as his wine (i.e., poison) server, a person that can have a double-meaning of being also himself, by the way, since his act was, after all, a suicide. In fact, in deeper esoteric meanings of Saqi in Persian poetry, the Saqi who is appealed to for serving Wine is actually not someone outside the "Tavern" of one's self, but one of the higher selves and voices within. So, the notion that appealing to a Saqi is necessarily an appeal to someone other than oneself would be wrong. It could be, but does not have to be, and can be both. In a poem where the poet is contemplating suicide, ultimately, the poisonous wine is being served by himself, whether aided by another or not.

- In light of the above interpretation, the second part of this main line of the code under the double lines is basically the expression (O Saqi). However, since the word can also be intended as a proper name, or a word that has multiple meanings, it is also correct to maintain and use TSM's own wording in the decoding as well, given he himself has allowed this by hinting with his double-lines, since it may have significance also as his own last or nickname, even though he may be also referring to his wine-server.

- In Persian poetry it is an established tradition for the poet to refer to himself by name in the poem, serving as a poet's signature. After all, broadly speaking, this is a suicide attempt, and it is he himself who is serving himself the poison, even when assisted by another. So, it may as well, and most likely, be the case that TSM is calling himself by his own name here, in the context of contemplating serving himself his own suicide drink.

- In an added interpretation, referring to the female wine-server as such may indicate an aspiration to call her by his own last name, as if in a wishful marriage proposal or ceremony, even though obviously nothing as such could be fulfilled. If he had a child with her, this poetic use of the word can be sadly meaningful that way. Beside, the female wine-server could have also been an "errand girl" involved in the spying trade, so the use of the term can have an added "double-meaning" significance.

- Therefore, the word AIAQC is so multiply meaningful in the code that it can serve simultaneously as a proper or nickname, as a reference to a water or wine (or in this case the poison) server implying another person and/or himself, to a spy in himself and/ or another person, to a dancer (and/or dance partner), and even in the context suggesting a family name used for the female server as his aspired wife who could have been also a spy and the mother of his child, if he lived and they were married. If so, calling her by his own last name (such as in how Jessica adopted Thomson's last name), the code may be even poetically regarded as a sadly unfulfilled or unfulfillable marriage proposal to or contract with her before dying, as if regarding the mother of his child his wife carrying his own last name, clearly rendering the code even more as a sad love poem.

- The second word of the third main line that is AB unambiguously stands for أب meaning father or dad or daddy, as shown here[49]. If you have wondered why in TSM's code there are many appearances of AB, it is because twice he uses it for the meaning "father" and "dad" or "daddy" and the word ABD for ابد happens also to start coincidentally with those two letters.

- The first word of the main third line of the code is MLI ملی or ملیء (the latter uses a hamzeh rendering of ya) can mean "fill" or "full" in Arabic as in here[50] or here.[51] This word may have its roots in Persian, since Persians are familiar with this term often used in poetry in a different rendering, when for example they say a cup was filled to the brim (مالامال).

- Overall in the third main line of the code, TSM is borrowing the "Saqi" or wine-server/wine-tender metaphor from Khayyam's poetry, insightfully characterizing his being served poison in terms of drinking his (last) wine. The line thus can read as, "Fill dad to the brim, O Saqi Ayaqçi" which should more properly retain the last word as a proper name. In other words, since the multiple meanings of Ayaqçi includes its being used as a proper name, we should keep it in the line as such as well in its both "double" senses; and here we can arrive at last at the significance of the double lines over the O AIAQC.

- If we have a poem that includes the word Khayyam, for example, it would be wrong to ignore the fact that it is being used as a proper name as well, rather than translating it only as a tent-maker. In a poetic context, both meanings can be intended, such as in "Khayyam who stitched his tents of wisdom." If we translate that line as "The tent-maker who stitched his tents of wisdom," ignoring "Khayyam" as a proper name, we would lose a lot in its translation as far as the reference to someone with that proper name is concerned. For the same reason, the best way we can respect TSM's rendition of this line of his code, given he even emphasized it himself with the double-lines, is to use the expression "O Saqi Aiaqçi." The nuances of TSM's use of the word AIAQC in his code would be ignored if we do not consider the multiple or at least the double meanings the word has.

- The word AIAQC is TSM's master brush stroke as a poet in his code. With one word he has skillfully conveyed a whole series of meanings. He is actually making himself known in the code, by offering that name, either as his actual name, or the nickname he would have liked to be called by, especially given the word essentially connotes as well references to "foot" and "dancing." Even the "x" may signify the wide variety of multiple meanings associated with the word below the double lines.

- Now we have a better sense of what the double-lines and the 'x' can signify on the third main line of TSM's code. Their being drawn over the expression O AIAQC with the 'x' on top of O not only can mean the multiple meanings associated with that word, but also we can make a strong case that the word is also in fact the last name of TSM, or at least the nickname by which he wished to be called. We should again not forget that the word AIAQC could also have the connotation of the "last dancer" for TSM in the context of the poem, as commonly understood in the Azerbaijani ancient dance of Yalli, whose style basically shares a lot in common with other Caucasian dances in the region, including Dagestan's Lezginka.

- Note: While it is tempting to consider MLIAB O AIAQC as the full name of TSM (ملیاب ا ایاقچی), MLIAB or ملیاب does not appear to be a widely common first name in Arabic, even though one can find folks named as ملیاب on the web. Just offering a full name as a complete line of the code does not fit well with the notion of the code's trying to offer a narrative beyond just a name. Otherwise, TSM could have simply signed his code off with that name or line.

10. The Second Main Line of the Code

The second main line of the code is comprised of the following: W TBI MPAN ETP

- The first letter/word W is a و for "and" or "with" or "while" (see here[52], where GT also uses W to transliterate the word). Although it is not separated in the code with a space from the next word TBI, this does not compromise or change the meaning of the next letter at all. It is possible in Arabic for و (W) to be joined with the next letter. We should also consider it possible that the W's ambiguity may have to do with its having been crossed-out. So, if interpretation allows, we can ignore the W.

- The second word, TBI, stands for طبی which means "medical" or medicine related (see here[53] or here[54]). The T used here in Arabic is ط (not the regular ت) which in Arabic transliteration is usually represented by a dot below the T as in Ṭ . Upon zooming, one can see a dot below T in the code's image, but that may be just a random marking or a coincidence. We don't know if TSM did that, given what we have is a tracing (by a police officer) of faint code markings. But the faintness of the dot may have to do with the later lack of tracing it, so it may have actually existed in the original faded writing (given it is still noticeable). The police officer did not of course know about the Arabic transliteration nature of the code, so he or she may have just ignored tracing that dot under the T. In any case, a dot is there and still visible.

- Since we have already established that the operating language of the code is Arabic, there is no reason to doubt that TSM meant to say طبی which transliterates as TBI. With a regular T as in ت the word would be a transliteration of تبی which GT translates as "she wants" in Arabic and in the context of the rest of the line as offered below it would not add anything specific or meaningful.

- The next word of the line is MPAN (considering ETP separately later). The P in the word has been regarded as ambiguous because of its larger than normal curve, and also the odd thin line inside it in the corner. As previously noted briefly, what most likely explains this is the following. In Arabic alphabet, there is no letter پ which in Persian alphabet stands for P. For this reason, in Arabic it is usually substituted and pronounced as B or F (for example see how in GT the proper names Pope, Peter Sampras, and Portugal are rendered in Arabic here[55], as Baba Alfatican, Bitir Sambras, and Bortugal, where Ps are substituted with Bs; this is one reason we even have Farsi for Parsi or Persian, since Farsi is an Arabized rendering of the word which has actually entered Persian language as well). TSM may have been trying to write P which does not exist in the Arabic alphabet, but first wrote it with a small circle on top, then realized to be consistent with writing capital letters, he should capitalize it also, so he ended up rewriting a larger curve as if capitalizing P. However, the fact that it is rendered unusually that way still offers a clue that TSM may not have been native in English, though he spoke and read English as well to some extent.

- If we remain consistent with the Arabic transliteration rule of decoding the third main line of the code, we should remember that in Arabic, there is no letter P. So, this seeming "anomaly" of finding a P in the code itself points to the likelihood that TSM was sharing an English proper word or abbreviation that includes P. Given the reference to medical prior to the word, we can then plausibly consider that indeed he is sharing the medical abbreviations for an illness. In that case, if we choose to regard the last letter of the line as a P also, and not a D, we would be led to consider that even ETP is also being offered as a medical abbreviation for an expression referring to his medical condition.

- It is really not out of place to offer medical information in the context of a poem meant to be a suicide contemplation note. One can even consider the possibility that having his Khayyam poetry booklet by his side on a hospital bed, where he is diagnosed with something using abbreviated medical terms, he could simply use the medical expression in his poem being jotted on the last page while thinking of how to end his suffering by suicide. If TSM was concerned about how others, including his future grown-up child for example, could understand why he committed suicide while having a new born child, it makes sense to give some hints about his assumed-to-be terminal illness making suicide justifiable or necessary in his mind, especially if he was subject to significant pain and suffering. If TSM was concerned that others may be misled to think that he did not love life and just wanted to die, then having a medical explanation for what led to his decision would be most appropriate, even in a poetic expression. If he was fed up with his terminal illness and wanted to make a statement about being reduced to a medical case label such as MPAN and/or ETP, his including it in the poem can be itself a way of depersonalizing and de-objectifying himself as a patient. This can even explain why he ends up, in the following line of the code (which we have already examined), offering in a poetic way his own proper name or preferred nickname.

- The abbreviation MPAN is presently associated with the rare neurological disease "Mitochondrial membrane protein-associated neurodegeneration (MPAN)" involving brain iron accumulation resulting in severe external and gait symptoms. But these symptoms were NOT found in TSM during autopsy; he was found to be actually quite fit physically and his brain was deemed normal, and given his poem, he must have also been sound in mind. More information about this disease can be found here[56] and also elsewhere online. If TSM's MPAN (as noted above) disease had reached such a point of severity that would have made suicide plausible, he would have had severe physical difficulties of even traveling to Adelaide by himself. So, it is very unlikely that what is known today as MPAN as noted above had anything to do with TSM's prior illness. Besides, such an abbreviation for that illness seems to be more recent than TSM's time. Medical experts of course are best qualified to comment on the above considerations based on TSM's autopsy results.

- What seems more probable is that the abbreviation refers to what used to be called Polyarteritis Nodosa as described here[57]. The following synopsis for the disease is offered online:

> "In 1923, Friedrich Wohlwill described two patients with a "microscopic form of periarteritis nodosa", which was distinct from classical polyarteritis nodosa. This disease, now known as microscopic polyangiitis (MPA), is a primary systemic vasculitis

characterized by inflammation of the small-caliber blood vessels and the presence of circulating antineutrophil cytoplasmic antibodies (ANCA)." (Source[58])

"Microscopic polyangiitis (MPA) is a condition that causes small blood vessels to be inflamed. It's a rare type of vasculitis. The disease can damage the blood vessels and cause problems in organs around the body. MPA most often affects people in their 50s and 60s, but it can happen in people of any age." (Source[59])

- Regarding the Microscopic Polyangiitis the information below is also offered online:

    "The first description of a patient with the illness now known as microscopic polyangiitis (MPA) appeared in the European literature in the 1920s. The concept of this disease as a condition that is separate from polyarteritis nodosa (PAN) and other forms of vasculitis did not begin to take root in medical thinking, however, until the late 1940s. Even today, some confusing terms for MPA (e.g., "microscopic poly *arteritis nodosa*" rather than "microscopic poly *angiitis*") persist in the medical literature. Confusion regarding the proper nomenclature of this disease led to references to "microscopic polyarteritis nodosa" and "hypersensitivity vasculitis" for many years. In 1994, The Chapel Hill Consensus Conference recognized MPA as its own entity, distinguishing it in a classification scheme clearly from PAN, granulomatosis with polyangiitis (GPA, formerly Wegener's), cutaneous leukocytoclastic angiitis (CLA), and other diseases with which MPA has been confused with through the years." (Source[60])

    "MPA can affect individuals from all ethnic backgrounds and any age group. In the United States, the typical MPA patient is a middle-aged white male or female, but many exceptions to this exist. The disease may occur in people of all ages, both genders, and all ethnic backgrounds." (Source[61])

- Therefore, it is possible that by the late 1940s the disease would have been referred to with an abbreviation such as MPAN, given the word "nodosa" at the end.

- This (second) "MPAN" (or how it is today referred to more correctly as MPA) disease as described above involves small sized vessels becoming enflamed, a condition called vasculitis, resulting in severe damage to internal organs, which can vary from patient to patient. TSM's own personal eating or drinking habits, such as drinking alcohol and smoking may have also contributed to worsening such a pre-existing condition. Because it is microscopic and defused through the body, the condition is not easily visible as a local vascular condition and would not be easily detectable in an autopsy perhaps, but its effects on internal organs will be readily apparent. Its symptoms and age occurrence seems to fit TSM's profile, a rare disorder that can also result in or worsen liver disease and contribute to enlargement of the spleen (called today splenomegaly) in some patients. Given the vasculitis condition, it may even explain TSM's dying from heart attack despite autopsy diagnosis of a healthy heart once also shocked by the intervention of poisoning. The shock may have ruptured or blocked the already enflamed veins leading to and from the heart.

- The study here[62] reports splenomegaly (enlargement of the spleen) not common but still present in few cases of the groups studied who were afflicted with Polyarteritis Nodosa (search for "splenomegaly" in the document). This[63] study can also be considered. For further considerations see also here[64].

- In case none of the above considerations for the illness are found to be relevant for TSM, it would still be helpful for medical experts to inquire further what the abbreviations given on this line reveal about TSM's illness. Given the reference to "medical" issues on this line, and given the fact that the letters used do not fit the Arabic transliteration rule (P not existing in Arabic alphabet), it is likely TSM was conveying some facts about his illness here. After all, leaving a suicide contemplation or planning note makes offering clues about the illness that made it necessary in the person's view relevant. For those trying to understand what TSM suffered from medically, MPAN ETP can be an interesting clue for further (including DNA) research.

- If we consider that the main second line of the code ends with a P and not a D, since P is not included in Arabic alphabet, we should then consider the medical diagnosis abbreviation to continue after MPAN, including ETP. The latter could have a variety of connotations, one of which that can fit TSM's context is "Eventually Terminal Patient." The notion "Eventually Terminal Illness" is a common expression for those suffering from an incurable disease and given there is no other word in the line except "medically," it is possible that TSM was here addressing a situation all patients face, which is that of being called not by a name but by being reduced to their medically diagnosed label.

- Regarding the last word of the line as ETP, if it is regarded to have ended with a D and not a P, it would stand for عتد which unambiguously means "be ready" or "prepare" as defined here[65]. In that case, TSM was using E to transliterate ع . Again, if we abide by the transliteration rule of the code, we should not expect E to represent a diacritic, but an actual letter, which would do so in that case. Nowadays the symbol ʿ is used for this letter in Arabic transliteration. However, the word E and ع are similar in capital rendering of E and the latter is even at times used for transliteration of the letter, such as for the word Ismaeil اسماعيل .

- The main second line of the code, therefore, basically offers the medical information for the illness TSM suffered from. However, in the context of the overall code, the line can be expressing facts that lead to the call for becoming prepared for the action to be taken as expressed in the following lines of the code (one which we have already examined, including the act of poisoning).

- If TSM had been suffering from a long-standing terminal illness, and had been hospitalized and/or medically diagnosed, he could have been given a name for his disease, and the simplest way the illness could have been remembered by him, especially if he was a migrant non-native in English language, was by its abbreviation.

- The illness may also explain why TSM ended up not having the expected vomiting symptoms from poisoning (even though he must have known and/or been told that was bound to happen following poisoning and he was expecting it, as sadly evident from the first line of the poem/code he left behind, to which we shall turn soon) given his death must have occurred suddenly due to blood blockage from and to the heart before the poison's effects could manifest themselves. Only medical experts can judge the relevance of thee above conjecture.

- Again, imagine a terminal patient on a hospital bed, with a copy of *The Rubaiyat* nearby dealing with matters of life and death, contemplating suicide and jotting down a plot for it, while being referred to medically as a MPAN eventually terminal patient. So, here, in a suicide plot, sketching a poem in which he can also make a reference to the illness from which he is suffering as a nameless patience, he incorporates a line reflecting that sentiment.

- In more recent years the letters ETP have been associated with leukemia (as in Early T-cell Precursor), which can also result in splenomegaly (enlargement of spleen); for example, consider this[66] study. It is not clear such an abbreviation would have been used in late 1940s, and on this medical historians are best qualified to comment, so, it can be further studied along that line.

- Again, in the context of a poem including a medical abbreviation explaining a suicide solution, it makes sense to find TSM using the medical label to hint at why he was contemplating suicide at the time. If TSM expected the illness to prevent him from ever dancing again in one way or another, it makes his plotting his departure as his "last dance" also more plausible.

- Overall, medical experts are best qualified to determine whether and how MPAN (as noted above), ETP, or a similar illness could have contributed to TSM's condition and decision to commit suicide, also further explaining his suicide symptoms. The Arabic transliteration environment of TSM's code points to the expressions having P as being proper names or abbreviations standing for technical terms. The way and place were the two Ps are placed in the expression MPANETP rule out the expression (after W TBI) being regular Arabic words. Of course if we regard the Ps as Ds then other efforts can be made to interpret the line, but it appears those letters were meant to be Ps.

11. The Crossed-Out Line of the Code

The crossed-out line of the code MLIAOI can be considered as MLI AOI or MLIA OI: ملى اوى or ملیا أى . The line is presumably left incomplete and is crossed-out, to be incorporated with changes in the third main line of the code.

- Since this line was crossed out, regarding its exactness or meaning we cannot make any definitive judgment. The reason TSM crossed it out to be later used with changes in the code's third main line may have to do partly with the space after M, which is corrected/eliminated on the third main line of the code. But, then, again, TSM did not seem to be trying to be word-spacing correct, given he did not strictly follow that requirement in the rest of his code. In this case, however, M by itself did not mean anything, so eliminating the space after it may have been considered necessary.

- Another reason the crossed-out line was crossed out could be that TSM found it necessary to add a B after A and before O, so the space between A and O was too tight to do so.

- The word ملیا in Arabic can mean "for a while," or "for a long time" in GT translation options here[67]. It can be verified further in the Arabic-English dictionary here[68]. In that case the next "word" can be an emotional expression such as "Oh" or "Ah" expressed in Russian as "oi" as in here[69].

- If we render the crossed-out line as MLI AOI or ملى اوى the word مَلى can still mean for a long time as in here[70], with the added advantage that the new word would be اوى which has a definite meaning of "accommodating" or "harboring" meaning as can be seen here[71]. So, it is possible to interpret the crossed-out line as meaning "for a long time harboring" which would be relevant to the next second main line of the code which refers to a medical condition. In that case, the crossed-line can add the notion of "having for a long time harbored ..." to the medical condition specified on the next line.

- It is possible to consider that the reason TSM crossed out this line was that he was faced with the challenge of fitting many expressions and ideas on one line, trying to maintain the quatrain form of the poem having a certain number of intended syllables for its meter. So, he was finding it difficult to fit the notions of "having for a long time harbored" or "for a long time, Oh ..." with the actual facts he was intending to give about his medical condition. Finding it impossible, he may have concluded that just making a reference to "medically" followed by his diagnosis label will suffice as the second main line of the poem. This then led him to incorporate the emotional "O ..." element differently in the third main line of the code (we examined earlier). This also can mean the similarity of MLIA or MLI from the crossed out line to the MLI in the third main line was just coincidental, since TSM used MLI in the third main line in its meaning as "fill" in relation to the Saqi trope.

- In hermeneutics, what is left out and is silent can be as important as what is stated. In this context, just because TSM crossed out the line does not render it useless for our interpretation. On this line, he seems to have been trying to express something, emotionally, about having endured a trouble for a long time, and this is why in the following main line of the poem he expresses some facts about his medical condition. So, in our overall interpretation of the code we should not necessarily ignore what was being conveyed in the crossed-out line.

12. The First Main Line of the Code

The first main line of the code is comprised of W RGO AB ABD.

- The first letter W has been considered ambiguous, to be either an W or an M. In Arabic W can transliterate as و (which can mean "and" or "with" or "while") but M would not mean anything other than being just a letter. Given the space after W, it is most likely a W. Generally, in the code wherever Ms are intended, they are written clearly. So, there is no reason to assume an ambiguous letter is an M, so it is safe to consider that it is most likely a W. The Arabic language and its transliteration rule of the code allows for W used as و in the two lines beginning with them.

- So, W stands for و meaning "and" or "with" or "while." Whether it is joined with or without space to the next word does not really make any difference in terms of meaning. But, if TSM intended to render the code as a poem, there are stylistic preferences we can consider. You can certainly start a poem's line with "And." If in writing and reciting a poem the number of syllables and its meter are important, even adding an "and" in the beginning can serve a function. In FitzGerald's translations of Khayyam, we find many quatrains that begin with "And"—for example, see quatrain numbers 3, 6, 8, 15, 19, 22, 42, 47 and 56 in the same edition TSM used; so TSM would have plenty of examples from FitzGerald to draw on to defend, say for his friendly English tutor in Jessica Harkness, his starting his suicide poem with an "And"!

- RGO in Arabic transliteration stands for رغو meaning unambiguously "foam" and "foaming" in Arabic (see here[72] or in the dictionary here[73]). Foaming is a less graphic and more "polite" way of referring to vomiting, befitting a poetic context. Besides, it has the double-meaning of expressing anger, such as our foaming or spitting at something. In Persian (and Arabic), the word for vomiting is استفراغ which is from the same root, but would be somewhat crude to use in a poem. The word استفراغ is familiar to any Arabic or Persian speaker. In this case, TSM is being poetically tactful in language while using double-meanings to express something important.

- Note how TSM correctly transliterated the words و as W for "and"

and و in رغو as O. The reason is the two letters sound different in the two contexts, in the former it sounds as in "wind" and in the latter as in "boy." This again suggests TSM was versed in Arabic and its transliteration protocols, and that he had a sound mind.

- AB stands for اب or اُب which refers to "father" or "dad" or similar words such as "daddy" (see here[74] or here[75]).

- ABD stands for ابد meaning "eternity" or "forever" (see here[76] or also here[77]). This word is so common in Arabic and Persian (and Turkish) that does not require further explanation. However, it is also used in context sometimes to imply never, as if expressing a "forever not," as in absolutely not. We should note that if TSM meant it in the latter sense, he would have had to add an Alif at the end to make possible the rendering ابدا . However, a diacritic may also do the job, so the word retains a double meaning with the more likely meaning intended being that of forever. In a poetic context, a poet can play with the double-meaning of the word. In this case, TSM is also offering a poetic master stroke here by implying multiple, even contradictory, meanings in the same words in the line. The "forever" could relate to both fatherhood and to foaming. And both could imply being forever, or never.

- Basically, in the first line of the code (even not adding any diacritics) و رغو اب ابد TSM is saying "And foam father forever." Of course, one can argue the forever refers to the father (as if wishing to be a father forever), but it can also mean a father that forever foams, imaginatively speaking, or in terms of actual foaming, or being angry at something. Foaming can also have the meaning of spitting at something, which connotes both anger and an emotional expression of rejecting something abhorred. Spitting at something as a sign of damning it is a common expression.

- We do not have full sentences in the code, so various interpretations can be made, with the most likely being that of TSM expressing an emotion by a father of foaming forever at and being angry at something. If you were a father who found himself having to commit suicide despite having a newborn child, would you not be foaming (and spitting) at the situation forever? Moreover, the foaming can relate to the expectation of TSM that he would be vomiting, or foaming, following the in-take of poison.

- So, the first line of the code seems to be actually quite a sad but creative, poetic, expression of a father who is contemplating dying from poisoning himself and being deprived of helping his son grow up and uses the expected foaming and spitting effects of the poisoning as a way of expressing his anger at his terminal illness that will end his chance of seeing his child again. This sounds like a sad but highly talented poetic mind at work.

- Notice that in the transliteration of غ TSM correctly uses the letter G. This indicates he is consistent with his application of the Arabic transliteration rules. The use of ق for G here would not produce any meaningful results.

- The first line of the code further reveals TSM as being himself either a poet, or one with refined poetic and dramatic sensibilities, finding himself amid a deeply sad and tragic situation, expressing in just a few words what it would be like to be found, as a father, foaming and vomiting from ingested poison. Still he is expressing it in a way that emphasizes he will forever be a father for his child he will miss raising. He was perfectly dressed for the occasion as a father, even if he was not used to it, preferring to wear the shirt coat in his suitcase instead. He polished his shoes the best he could, wore his best cloths (even if bought used), for his last good-bye. He acted out his poem, even dancing for death, with his legs crossed, his right hand folded over and played around "in a funny way" which could have actually been gestures amid his last dancing moves, with 'Tamám Shud' clip in his fob pocket.

- All this is telling of a deliberately acted out performance, of a last dance meticulously enacted on a public stage. Given what transpired on the global stage, it seems TSM (along with his quietly dancing-along partner) was an imaginative artist involved in dramatic arts. Jessica Thomson could have revealed what happened in 1948 any time before she died in 2007 (not knowing of course that their child would die two years later). But she too seems to have remained committed to the act's secret plot instruction of "keeping distance" and to her and TSM's love story dance ending while having fulfilled both their wishes.

13. Interpreting the Code as a Whole

In Arabic transliteration conversion using a more or less standard table, the code can be unambiguously and predictably converted to the basic Arabic (and the few Roman) letters and groupings below (read from right to left when reverted back into Arabic, of course, except for the medical case label that still reads left to right), without any need for adding diacritics to arrive at the basic structure of the text in Arabic. In other word, TSM consistently does not include diacritics in his transliteration (which proves that it is not a transliteration from Turkish, whose script includes diacritics):

و رغو اب ابد

(ملیا وی)

و طبی "MPAN ETP"

ملی اب اُه ایاقچ

ات تمت سام ست غاب

To simplify things, we will just set aside the option of the second main line ending with D (that is, set aside the ETD option), and just follow the generally accepted reading that the last letter was a P and not a D. If we read the last letter of the second main line of the code (following the crossed-out line) as a D, ETD would transliterate as عتد , meaning "make ready!" or "prepare!" as can be see here[78]. Those who wish to consider that possibility in their interpretations of the code, they can, and it will not violate the overall meaning of the code. It will take away the option of regarding ETP as a medical term or information, if that is what was intended. But "prepare" or "make ready" would also fit in with the other lines of the poem, as if TSM is preparing himself for his Saqi to serve the poison.

However, considering the last letter of the second main line as P can also fit with the intention TSM may have had for that line, referring to his medical label as an "MPAN ETP" as if saying "MPAN Eventually Terminal Patient." It is possible that as a hospital patient, or being medically diagnosed, such a label was used for him or included in his chart, or conveyed to him by, say, a nurse in Jessica, as what medical doctors could call his case.

It is important to keep in mind that the code contains minimal words as code word hints, not necessarily being intended to offer grammatically completed full sentences. It is also important to note that in any poem, even when normally expressed, some words can have many meanings, and TSM seems to have been skilled at it poetically and intended to use the strategy to express many meanings in a short code.

In other words, even if you have a poem in any language, you can endlessly argue what it means and how to translate it, and Khayyami scholars and enthusiasts of course know that story. So, just because we have decoded the code as being rendered in Arabic transliteration system, which is really the most significant overall discovery being reported in this research report, this does not mean we could not explore all the various ways the poem can be interpreted and translated. Still, it will be shown below that the code can be interpreted unambiguously in its overall meaning.

Omar Khayyam's quatrains are known for their ability to condense deep and profound philosophical meanings in simple few words and lines, so TSM must have clearly taken inspiration from Khayyam here.

The dominant literal meaning of the words in the code can be unambiguously arrived at as in the following, the alternative meanings added in parenthesis; for our translation, we will focus on the meanings conveyed in dominant ways, but also consider the crossed-out line, as TSM did, allowing for its meanings to be implied in the final poetic code's expression. Remember, these are hint words, not full grammatically expressed sentences. The bracketed line is the one crossed-out in the original code:

- And/to foam or foaming/father/forever (or never)
- [For a long time/Ah] or [For a long time harboring]
- With (and, or while, or related term, or can be ignored) medically (implying medically diagnosed)/MPAN ETP (if the last letter is a D and last word ETD, then ETD can stand for "make ready!")
- Fill/father or dad/O Saqi/Aiaqçi
- It's done (she completed it)/poisonous/lady/evade or keep distance (with a hint of "you'll be missed")

The poetic code itself, as found in TSM which basically offers hint words in its Arabic rendering, seems to be comprised of about 8 syllables for each line's meter. TSM was trying to express feelings and thoughts he could not fit in that meter scheme, leading him to cross out few words.

FitzGerald's rendering is usually in 10 syllables for each line, so it offers us more meter spacetime for a possible translation. However, FitzGerald, as much as he could himself fit things in a 10-syllable meter, caused unnecessary hardships for generations of translators by that 10-meter scheme, which he must have deemed more suited for his British audience.

Khayyam, for wonderful reasons to be explained in the 12-book *Omar Khayyam's Secret* series (Okcir Press, 2021-), chose a 12 syllable meter structure for his poems. So, even though TSM was holding a FitzGerald translation of Khayyam at hand and was perhaps expecting a translation in its meter, let us render his code in all 8-, 10-, and 12-syllables rhyme in English translations, including the latter way the poet Omar Khayyam preferred to express his thoughts. Besides, this offers us more meter spacetime to include all the essential, multiply-connotated, meanings TSM seems to have intended to convey in his last words.

The second line includes a poetically condensed expression for "medical diagnosis as a MPAN Eventually Terminal Patient." If ETP itself stands also for an illness, then, the abbreviation can still accommodate that meaning. If ETP is replaced by ETD, it would mean "make ready." The doubling of Aiaqçi as explicitly coupled with Saqi is supported by TSM's double lines markings on the top of the word, with 'x' also suggesting the central role the multiply-meaningful Aiqaçi plays in the poem as a whole.

Were we to express the above elements rhymed as a quatrain minimally as in the code (8 syllables meter), it would be something like the first version below. Expanded to 10 and 12 syllables, the notions intended in the crossed-out line and a second implicit meaning of "missing someone" in GAB can also incorporated (the crossed-out line offers the notion of a long time in either reading, and the expression Ah or 'harboring').

In an 8-syllables meter version, which matches that found in TSM's Arabic original, we can have the following (MPAN and ETP should be read as 2- and 3-syllable words respectively, as in M-PAN and E-T-P):

And foam, father, eternally,
At illness "MPAN ETP"!
Fill dad, O Saqi Aiaqçi!
Poisoning done, evade lady!

In an expanded 10-syllables meter version, which would match the meter usually used by FitzGerald in translation, we can have the following:

> *And be foaming, father, eternally,*
> *At your illness case "MPAN ETP"!*
> *Fill for daddy, O Saqi Aiaqçi!*
> *Poisoning done, keep a distance lady!*

An expanded 12-syllables meter version, the meter followed by Omar Khayyam in his original Persian, allows for incorporating feelings and thoughts TSM may have been trying to include as found in the crossed-out line. So, we can have the following to convey the basic spirit of what and how TSM was trying to express:

> *And to foam, Ah father, for an eternity*
> *At your long diagnosis "MPAN ETP"*
> *Fill daddy to the brim, O Saqi Aiaqçi!*
> *Poisoning done, keep distance, you'll be missed lady!*

Were we to use diacritics (in lower case below) in the Arabic transliteration of TSM's original code so that non-Arabic speakers could read the poem more fluently (rather than as a series of consonant letters), to gain a sense of its meter and rhyme, it would sound something like the following (again, read the illness abbreviation as M-PAN E-T-P):

> *Wa RaGO ABi ABaDi*
> *Wa TeBI MPAN ETP*
> *MALI ABi O AIAQÇi*
> *IT TaMaT SAM SeTo GABi*

For Persian readers, given Khayyam's book has been used in drafting the code, TSM's poem could be translated in its spirit as follows:

و تُفی کُن ابدی، آه پدر،

بر مرض شریانی درازمدت و بی درمانت!

پُر کن بابا را مالامال ای ساقی اِیاقچی!

سَمّ تمام شد دوری جو خانم، دلتنگت خواهم شد!

The code's deciphering clearly establishes that: 1) TSM knew or assumed he had fathered a child (a son) with Jessica Thomson (regarding an alternative wider story, we will comment later); 2) He had suffered from a long-standing illness perceived by him to be terminal; 3) He intended to commit suicide by poisoning; 4) He intended to meet Jessica Thomson for a last visit to see also his son, offering her the gift of his *Rubaiyat* copy signed by his own transliterated suicide note, reminding her that she should keep distance from others following his death. The latter part of the plot is actually quite central and critical for his plan of a mysterious departure, and it appears that Jessica Thomson remained committed to her "evasion" plot to her end as well.

However, we should keep in mind that the poem was a suicide *contemplation and plotting* note on TSM's part, the content of which (even the poem itself) TSM may have discussed with Jessica earlier during the affair they had. But, this does not mean that it was actually known to her as such, drafted on the back of a Khayyam poetry booklet, and given he may not have succeeded in seeing her on his last day, he did not get a chance to give her the booklet and the poem directly on the day he died.

So, she may not have been herself aware of the role she was expected (by TSM) to play on that day, as far as serving or aiding poison is concerned. Alternatively, it is possible that Jessica knew of TSM's plan, but could not bring herself to the point of being present when he took the poison or play a part in the act, her being absent at her home being interpreted as a rejection or lack of her interest in participation by TSM. Given that we know now what the code meant, and he did not leave it with Jessica, instead tossing it in a car, that is itself an important indication that they did not actually meet on his last day for one or another reason. Otherwise, he could have simply given her the booklet in person.

But, this does not mean Jessica could not have discovered for herself what the code was about following his suicide. If she knew TSM well enough to know that he could speak and read Arabic, she could have readily learned for herself what the code meant as a translation from Arabic by way of consulting an Arabic dictionary. The key to the code's deciphering has basically been connecting the dots of 'Tamám Shud' as a transliteration from Persian based on Arabic alphabet (which Persian also uses) and the code as a transliteration from Arabic. Anyone who connects those dots and pursues the inquiry seriously, even if he or she is not versed in Arabic, can decipher the code. We will of course later ask why it is that for seven decades no one seriously considered this option despite hints some observers have offered regarding the code being a transliteration. Even so, such observers were thinking the translation is from Persian (like in 'Tamám Shud') and never considered it being from Arabic. Transliterating the code back to Persian actually does not produce any meaningful results.

TSM may have been a spy from the Arabic dialect speaking, Lezgi dancing, communities of the Caucasus' Dagestan, serving the last sip of his poetry's wine in the style of the great Omar Khayyam, to make himself like the centuries-old Persian master poet immortal in the memories of future generations. Besides having a sense of meticulous planning for his final assault on the enemy of his terminal illness in the form of a last dance of his life in the hopes of leaving behind a lasting puzzle to solve by others, it appears that he maintained his Khayyami sense of bittersweet sarcasm—even wit regarding the "evasion" instruction—to his end, hurling his eternal curse of foaming or spitting at his illness, playing metaphorically with the condition he expected to be found, that is, of having vomited due to poisoning, while being well-dressed for the public stage and prepared for his final act with postures that implied dancing moves.

He therefore creatively wove the idea of his foaming or vomiting curse into other facts leading to his suicide, himself assuming responsibility for the final act. He may have received inspiration (also by way of Jessica Thomson) from a recent suicide by George Marshall in the Sydney area using the *Rubaiyat* as a prop, but he decided to choreograph his departure differently (see here[79]).

Unfortunately, contrary to the spirit of Omar Khayyam who did everything he could in his life to live his life to the fullest amid his most troubling times, now having been discovered by OKCIR for the first time to have died a centenarian, born in AD 1021 and dead at the age of 102 in AD 1123 (see the first three volumes of OKCIR's *Omar Khayyam's Secret* series already published in 2021), his poetry has often been misunderstood as conveying a sense of nihilism and wish for death. Even a prominent, already depressed, Iranian writer, Sadegh Hedayat, known for his own interpretation of Khayyam's poems, took his own life in 1951, aged 48, in Paris (see here[80]).

TSM, contrary to George Marshall who seems to have suffered from mental illness, does not fit a model of Khayyam readers who commit suicide due to mental illness, and his act seems to have been deemed a necessary reaction to a perceived, imminent, terminal illness. And even his code for his choreographed suicide tells of a reluctance, implying spitting at the circumstances leading to suicide.

In any case, we should note that several events on his last day went somewhat differently from how he planned his departure.

First, a sadly pleasant irony of his final act was that his illness may have in fact helped in saving him from the vomiting symptom, which was intended to serve as an expected poetic prop as a curse involving eternally spitting at his illness. Or, perhaps he did indeed succeed at cursing at it, poetically speaking, by way of leaving his code (talking about the spitting) for generations to decipher. The transliterated word ABD, or ابد , can mean simultaneously (in Arabic, Persian or Turkish) as "forever" and "never," depending on the diacritics used. Was that word's double-meaning also intended to suggest that he may have suspected (or wished) that he may not eternally "foam" and spit as a curse at his illness due to his poisoning? It seems more reasonable that he expected to vomit as a result of poisoning, composing his poem around the theme. Otherwise, why even mention it, if he knew he was not going to vomit after all? It is doubtful that he would have found himself so much in control so as to determine whether he would vomit or not as a result of poisoning.

Second, it appears that contrary to his plans on his last trip to Somerton, which included meeting Jessica Thomson and his son for the last time, handing her his copy of *The Rubaiyat* with his transliterated signature poem (which also served as a reminder warning to her to lie low, evade others, and keep distance following it) on its back page, he could not meet her. This was either due to her deliberate rejection (which does not imply that she actually knew he was planning to commit suicide that day), or that she could not bring herself emotionally to play her part in the plot of aiding his suicide despite having views favoring euthanasia rights, or simply because she was not home. So, he walked around and tried again, and losing hope, he tore the 'Tamám Shud' piece to keep in his fob pocket, while tossing the book in a car nearby, perhaps as also a nod to her prospective husband being a used-car dealer, counting on it being eventually delivered one way or another to Jessica Thomson using the phone number on the back.

Since she had not been actively involved in his suicide plans that day, he was not concerned that she would be held responsible for his death, jeopardizing her life and her caring for their son. And she may not have even known or suspected of his having committed suicide until seeing his death bust. She may not have gifted him that *Rubaiyat* copy as she had done to Alf Boxall, so did not necessarily know the copy unearthed had anything to do with him particularly. So, she, like many others until today, may not have known what that code meant initially, but had plenty of time soon after until she died decades later to learn what it means, if she had a slightest hint that TSM knew Arabic and that the code could be a transliteration from Arabic. She may have assumed "those higher than the local police" knew TSM because he and she had been spies or at least suspected to be spies, because of their ideological and political leanings.

Given the circumstances, and being aware that she and he both may have been involved in spying, she assumed others knew him and knew what had happened. But what happened was simply a case of a terminally ill father who realized he could not raise his child and marry his Australian sweetheart, sadly ending his suffering with the intention of doing so poetically as a mysterious performance, having hoped to see his lover and their son one last time before dying.

The TSM code was basically a contemplated assisted suicide note, in which he meant to leave behind the above message. Given that his departure had been carefully contemplated, plotted, and performed it is not surprising that it started an international puzzle-solving spree in the coming decades, leading him to acquire a lasting life in global public imagination.

From the way he choreographed his departure, it seems he did intend to leave behind him a puzzle to solve, and to understand why, we will have to consider the relevance of Omar Khayyam to his case. After all, he could have written his poem on the back of any poetry book, so why Khayyam? To understand why we need to consider the relevance of Khayyam to his departure plan in a different light.

14. The Relevance of Omar Khayyam's *'Rubaiyat'*

It can be hermeneutically helpful for us to understand, aside from other personal interests TSM and Jessica Thomson may have had in Khayyam's poetry, why his case could have become entangled with the life and works of Omar Khayyam, especially the quatrains or the Robaiyat (or in FitzGerald's transliteration, 'Rubaiyat') attributed to him.

Those reporting on TSM have pointed to Khayyam's relevance to the man in terms of the poetry's subject dealing with matters of life and death and search for the meaning of life—that life is short, we must be aware of our mortality, and try to make the best of what's left of our lives, without any regrets left behind. This is generally true, of course, not only because matters of life and death are existential questions that confront all humankind, but also because for someone who is terminally ill and contemplating suicide in the shadow of a WWII such poetry could have had an immediate and deeper meaning.

However, we should also consider that we are dealing here with a situation where a person is seriously contemplating suicide. So, the intention here is not to cherish and prolong life, but to end it. For this reason, it is important to consider the relevance of Khayyam's work to the events in a broader and different light.

One aspect of TSM's association with the poetry of Khayyam that should be kept in mind is that Khayyam's poetry offers us all, as did TSM, a practical example of how someone can physically die but keep on living in spirit in the memory of later generations world-wide for a very long time. We have a case, in other words, of someone like Omar Khayyam who died centuries ago, but we know him and his works, and still read his poetry all over the world to this day.

If TSM was terminally ill and contemplating suicide, he had by his side in the form of Khayyam's poetry in FitzGerald's translation a proven example of how someone could physically die but continue living in spirit in others' memory for a long time—someone who produced a work of art in the form of poetry a long time ago in such a way that it could generate sufficient interest and curiosity in the mind of future generations such that he could become spiritually enduring in human memory.

So, if we put ourselves in the shoes of TSM's time following a devastating world war and his personal life afflicted with terminal illness, it would be plausible to consider that he could have been asking himself, and we could also ask ourselves: How did Khayyam do it? How did Khayyam write his poetry such that he has been remembered for so long and so widely down the generations?

This is a very interesting question, and of course those who are familiar with the life and works of Khayyam know that his interest in such matters was not tangential, but deep, serious, and lifelong. OKCIR's presently underway 12-book series under the common title *Omar Khayyam's Secret* is actually trying to answer that question more deeply, such that it cannot be shared in the limited space of this report. Khayyam had a passionate and enduring interest throughout his life in existential questions, specializing on matters of existence, of life and death, so to speak. In today's language, he was an "expert on existence" and on how to have a lasting spiritual life.

So he must have learned and done something right in the form of his life and works, especially in the form of his poetry, resulting in his becoming spiritually immortal across generations. FitzGerald himself became a lasting name in human memory (even considering that he self-published his own first edition anonymously, not selling for a while even for a penny, we must note) thanks to Khayyam. He did not become famous because of his translations of another Persian poet Farideddin Attar or other poets or authors he translated from other languages, but because of what meanings Khayyam was conveying in his poetry.

If TSM was terminally ill and suffering, and seriously contemplating suicide, apart from leaving behind an offspring, he must have also considered how he could plan his sooner than expected departure in such a way that could result in an enduring presence in others' memories after he died. Given the indications that he was creative, interested in poetry, and most likely a serious performance dancer as well, aside from being versed in matters of secrecy and code-writing due to having also had intelligence backgrounds or training, it is possible that he decided to choreograph the conditions of his suicide due to inevitable terminal illness in such a way that could result in generating perpetual curiosities about his identity, life, and death.

So, as he was reading his *Rubaiyat* and thinking about matters of life and death and meaning of life while confronting a terminal illness, he could have also imagined plotting his suicide's drama in such a way that could even be jotted down and expressed in a poetic style in the gist of a code written as a quatrain. He could have told himself basically, "I am going to die soon any ways, why not stage it as a public performance of what I loved the most in my life, dancing."

While we do not know the extent to which TSM deliberately planned on the idea of producing a suicide plot and poem in the form of a mysterious code for a similar end, even as brief as it is, trying to emulate Khayyam's art, what transpired on that day clearly gives the impression of a carefully planned plot. The fact of the matter is that how TSM arranged the circumstances of his demise during his final years and days ended up having results that parallel the effects Khayyam's poetry has had across generations.

Besides, he (and Jessica Thomson) had the example of another recent event, the suicide of George Marshall in Sidney, Australia, to draw upon, given the media and public attention the latter received. So, associating one's departure with Khayyam's example as a lasting spirit beyond physical death is something that could be sadly enticing for someone who knows he will die soon but wishes to continue living in spirit otherwise in others' memories. Whether you, the reader, like it or not, The Somerton Man is living in spirit through you and your interests in his case.

Considering the historical conditions of the times following WWII, of course The Rubaiyat could serve to remind us to appreciate the brief lifetime we all face, so it could have even served, say a Jessica Thomson, to encourage TSM not to commit suicide if he faced terminal medical conditions or other hardships in life. But, if doing so was a decision contemplated and decided on by TSM, because death was coming his way soon any ways due to his terminal illness, the poetry collection served also as a proven example of how he could also live in others' memory for a long time following physical death.

So, in response to the question why TSM went to such length of choreographing his suicide as a mysterious drama in favor of a lasting life in human memory, the answer may lie in his having found the possibility of such an outcome being already proven in the Omar Khayyam's poetry translation booklet on the back of which he wrote his code.

TSM was facing a terminal illness. It makes sense to consider him trying to emulate Khayyam, by leaving a message that would also make him last in the memory of later generations. Had Jessica Thomson immediately revealed after his death TSM's identity and the nature of what happened, the plot would have ended soon as just another suicide case, without her even having to worry about being implicated in it. But, she chose to stay committed to her "evasion" dance plot with TSM to her end as well. And this is why the very last word and instruction TSM gave wittingly in his poetic code, GAB or غاب , as odd and brief as it is, is so important and necessary for the success of the plot. Without her purposely "evading" and persistently "keeping distance" TSM's last dance with her would not have become lasting. TSM's dance physically ended on Dec. 1, 1948, but his spiritual dance along with that of Jessica proving her love for him lasted all her life and beyond it as well.

Caring for and still loving the Somerton man deeply can perhaps best explain why Jessica Thomson, the Somerton woman, played the part to her end in her solitude, for her own heart, through all those decades. She played the part despite knowing she would be accused of this or that regarding the Somerton man. All she had to do was to dance gently and quietly along and not "let it out of the bag" (as her daughter put it), letting him dance his more active part performing his suicide footwork. Her dance was as essential as that of the Somerton man to their plot. That is essentially how a Lezginka dance between a man and a woman is supposed to be traditionally played out:

> "Lezginka, also spelled Lezghinka, folk dance originating among the Lezgin people[81] of the Caucasus[82]. It is a male solo dance (often with a sword) and also a couple dance. The man, imitating the eagle, falls to his knees, leaps up, and dances with concise steps and strong, sharp arm and body movements. When the dance is performed in pairs, couples do not touch; the woman dances quietly as she regards the man's display." (Source[83])

15. The Wider Story

The TSM "code" served as a suicide contemplation and plotting note, not necessarily suggesting that he was actively assisted by a female aid for the poison/drug acquisition and/or administration. She may have generally known about the possibility, being aware of his medical and financially unstable condition as a migrant (which explains why she had already decided to raise the child on her own and by way of another more secure marriage). She may have even doubted, following their affair, his sincerity about following through with suicide given his terminal illness, thinking that perhaps he just wanted the affair and then left her traveling, not to hear back from again.

She may have even herself been, despite acknowledging his right to commit suicide and euthanasia, reluctant to take part in the plot to the extent of actively serving him the poison, since after all he was the father of her child. So, overall, that, or any of the other above reasons, may explain the distance between her and TSM before the eventful day. So, it would be understandable if she felt despaired or betrayed at some point, herself contemplating and trying to commit suicide, given the heavy responsibilities of giving birth to and raising the child on her own.

It is possible TSM and the nursing student met in a hospital setting a few years back when he was ill, and given his terminal condition she offered to help. Given the unlisted phone number TSM had on his book was of her latest residence following after her child's birth, it indicates that they must have been still in touch, or he had been trying to keep in touch, for a while.

Given no leads were found to TSM's identity, presumably even as a patient in nearby hospitals (if such data could have been made available at the time), it is also possible that the two were acquainted differently, perhaps as spy agents, through which he sought her help for his medical condition.

It is also likely, however, that their meeting each other took place while TSM was as a migrant being tutored English by Jessica Harkness, perhaps as a cover for their spying activities as well. Omar Khayyam's poetry could have served well as a textbook. In that context, her nursing skills and knowledge (to the extent available to her as a student) and his health condition could have been a subject of their conversation, given that he must have been suffering from the illness for a while and was contemplating how to heal it, or, alternatively, to end his suffering by committing suicide.

Jessica herself was suicidal following her pregnancy, so the right to end one's life may have been a subject of their conversations, both being in favor of euthanasia as a right. Having an affair leading to pregnancy could have been unplanned or intentional, but it could contribute as a way of continuing TSM's life by way of an offspring, in case he died naturally or by way of suicide (as a hypothetical possibility at the time when they had an affair). However, given the hardships Jessica would have to go through raising the child alone, it seems her pregnancy could not have been such a deliberate idea, even as a way of leaving a keepsake for an ill TSM. So, it may have been more likely an accidental conception.

Jessica Thomson is known to have regarded Khayyam's poetry as "love poetry," and used it to make friendships with others. But, this does not necessarily mean that the copy of *Rubaiyat* TSM possessed was also one gifted to him by Jessica. Perhaps even it was he who made her more interested in Khayyam than she would have been on her own, given his cultural background. In any case, when the police asked her about it, and not being yet aware of the dead man found being the person she knew, the first (and perhaps only) case she could recall was that of gifting a copy to Boxall. Given TSM himself was, as a Russian from the Caucasus, also familiar with Arabic (or trained in the latter), Khayyam's poetry must have had added meaning for him, even though the poems were composed originally in Persian; it is possible TSM may have even known Persian to some extent, given the Caucasus and Iran share common cultural and linguistic backgrounds by way, especially, of the Azeri cultural heritage.

For TSM, having had an affair with the nursing student, this was his last trip to see her and/or his infant son before committing suicide. In general, perhaps given she had not planned for his being involved in raising their child, given his health condition and limited means, and given her ambivalence about being a party to his poisoning in practical terms, she may not have been even eager in reestablishing contact. She was trying to keep distance even before TSM died, in other words, not letting the past disrupt the relatively more stable condition she needed to raise her child while being engaged to Mr. Thomson. So, she may not have wanted to be involved, let alone be implicated, directly in his death afterwards.

TSM's leaving her phone number (even in small writing) on the poetry book alongside the code, given how he intended to implement his poetic plan when giving it to her, indicates that at the time he simply planned to give her the copy in person as a keepsake. However, given they ended up not meeting, and given he knew she was not involved in his suicide, he did not have to worry about her being implicated in his death. By tossing the book in the car, he may have even had considered that it may end up reaching her following his death, but he may have also felt despaired and dejected in not having been able to meet her and his son on his last day. He must have planned carefully to have no money or anything else to survive on past that day, so performing the last act of the suicide plot had to be done, whether or not he succeeded in meeting her that day.

The Somerton Man could have been a Russian from Shirvani Arabic speaking Caucasian minorities in the Caucasus, or, someone who had been educated in using Arabic for communication or even as a coding technique. He did not seem to be a formally religious man, given he left no religious prayers in the code (unless we interpret "forever father" as referring to God, which does not make sense in relation to foaming, unless we interpret the first line as a curse against God; but such an interpretation does not fit well with the rest of the poem, given the "father" is used as a referent for preparing himself for his death).

He may not have been born Muslim, could have been a Christian such as an Armenian, or born in another religion, or held no religious beliefs, being atheist in orientation. TSM's cheaper cigarette box containing better quality cigarettes may actually be an indication of his trying to play the dramaturgical role of being a proletarian in relation to his spy contacts, while desiring a more pleasant smoking experience.

Sociologists can find in the Somerton Man case plenty of interesting elements to explore their Erving Goffmanian dramaturgical theories of sociology (treating everyday life as a performance stage), and Herbert Blumerian symbolic interactionists in sociology can study and illustrate their concepts by drawing on what transpired symbolically in the events leading and following the strange loving dance performance spanning decades between TSM and Jessica. Above all, The Somerton Man case can be an excellent case study in C. Wright Millsian sociological imagination, who was himself also socialist-oriented and critical-minded, trying to understand not only how personal troubles and public issues relate to one another, but how they can be and become at once one another in a dialectic that Jessica and TSM along with Mills would have shared an interest in, being all different and independent-minded thinkers.

It is possible TSM was from regions or locations in the former Soviet Union where people spoke Arabic, or was employed as an "errand boy" spy because of his skills including knowledge of Arabic language. He may have learned his Arabic transliteration skills as a literary, or someone trained in code-writing. He may have even participated as a member of the various Russian goodwill dance tours traveling to Europe, the U.S., Australia, and around the world, also choreographed them.

Given the autopsy reports of his not having been circumcised, it is likely he was not Muslim (or Jewish) by birth. Circumcision is not common among the Cossack community of the Caucasus, and Armenians are not religiously required to do so. He may have been raised in an ideologically leftist, atheist family, so was not subject to circumcision ritual as a child. TSM, if Russian, must have grown up during revolutionary turmoil and war conflicts in his homeland, losing most if not all his relatives amid such hardships.

If he was from the Caucasus, this should show in his DNA tests, if sufficient samples are found to yield definitive results. His DNA information that was revealed from analyzing his hair (haplogroup H4a1a1a) points to regions that also include the north Caucasus region (see H4 concentration in the northern Caucasus region here[84]). He was not necessarily from an established Arab nation, but from an Arabic speaking community in the broader Russian region.

Knowing Arabic well does not necessarily translate into someone being an Arab, but the extent and depth of the code's engagement with Arabic is telling of someone who was comfortable with using Arabic as a language to write his poetic suicide note as a code. But his decision to do so may have been prompted simply by his trying to emulate the 'Tamám Shud' example, and not being native in Persian, he chose to do so in Arabic with which he was more familiar. Even FitzGerald could have written such a code without being Persian or Arab, had he decided to write more than just 'Tamám Shud.'

Since all the autopsy results indicate that other than internal organ problems TSM was physically fit with signs of leg muscles indicating his having been seriously trained and involved in the dancing arts (resembling ballet), and given he was found to have unusually large hands, it would not be far-fetched to consider that he have been familiar with and skilled at dances of the peoples living in the Caucasus, such as Lezginka, including being trained in its acrobatic dance performances. Russian and Lezginka dances appear even to non-specialists to involve movements similar to ballet, that can result in leg and calf muscle features found in TSM, having fit body and hands.

If Mrs. Thomson's son was TSM's, given she must have known about his dancing skills, it is possible she may have encouraged her son to take up the art as an unspoken tribute to him, in the form of ballet that is more accessible in Australia than on the Caucasus mountains. There is even a photo of Jessica Thomson in a dancing pose. Who knows, she may have even shared a dancing shirt, socks, or boots, gifted by TSM to his son for when he grew up, without the latter necessarily knowing about his biological father's background, in light of her trying to keep the secret from even their son.

The trope AIAQC may have been (or could have become, if she was at home and/or had answered his knock on the door) a topic of discussion between TSM and his suicide aid, both having perhaps been interested or involved in code-writing and surely in *The Rubaiyat*. She did not have to know Arabic to be offered the poem and its meaning, as it could have been explained to her by TSM before taking the poison. Jessica possibly served as the migrant TSM's English tutor using *The Rubaiyat* as a textbook, and TSM not being native in English may have given added incentive to him to write it in the 'Tamám Shud' transliteration style, trying to impress her on his last day, by giving her his own long-used copy of *The Rubaiyat* (knowing she read Khayyam) with his signature poem in 'Tamám Shud' style inscribed lightly on its back.

The code and the suicide, however, seem to have had little to do with espionage or military intelligence matters per se, although one or both may have had such background and experience as well, and he may have decided to playfully render his last inevitable act in the form of a spying plot or intrigue. The secrecy in the form of its expression could have been intended to also serve to protect the identity of TSM's child's mother who had to raise the child evidently. If remotely she was implicated in the suicide, the code could have served to readily exonerate her (for which she could simply provide the decoding key, which is basically that it is of an Arabic alphabet transliteration construction like in 'Tamám Shud'). The transliterated 'Tamám Shud' torn-out piece in TSM's fob pocket clearly linked him to *The Rubaiyat* booklet on which the code was found.

It appears that TSM actually did not get a chance to speak to Jessica Thomson on his last day. Whether intentionally rebuffed or just being a matter of her not being home, he ended up just tearing the 'Tamám Shud' words to put in his fob pocket, tossing the booklet into an open-window car as a nod to her husband's used-car business, hoping that somehow it may end up reaching her, given the phone number. Whether or not he did so out of despair or to get back at her rejecting his last effort in reaching out to her, his tossing the book clearly served the purpose of others forever knocking on her door, had she not specifically requested from the police to "keep distance."

TSM may have interpreted her not being home (despite a prior call), or not opening the door as a sign of her continued rejection despite bearing and raising his child, so he may have had an incentive in letting others find the poetry book than leave it behind her door, to avoid its being found and tossed away by her prospective husband, or to be further rejected by her.

16. An Alternative and/or Additional Wider Story?

Let us suppose that the DNA analyses currently underway on TSM's exhumed body remains end up proving that he had nothing to do with any love affair with Jessica Thomson, nor with Robin Thomson being his son. Let us suppose that the results prove Robin to be Mr. Thomson's son actually, or from anyone other than the Somerton Man. Where would such results take us in understanding the meaning of the so-called "code" we have deciphered now, one we have to assume to have been actually the words of TSM?

The answer to the above question actually can point us to a topic which has hardly been raised and discussed regarding TSM. When he was found dead on the Somerton Park beach on Dec. 1, 1948, TSM was about 40-50 years of age. What was he doing before then, whether or not in his last years he became involved with a Jessica Thomson? Did he live in Australia? Was he living in and traveling from the US? Was he engaged in WWII in the Soviet Union or somewhere else in relation to its peoples and armies?

TSM was born before the October Revolution and before WWI. If he was born around 1905, he would have been a young teenager at the time of the October Revolution and WWI, and in 1941, a fully grown-up man to be recruited or somehow involved in WWII or its consequences. And, of course, this is all assuming that he was from the broader Russian region and the Caucasus.

Our findings regarding the meaning of the "code" can also point to a life-story before Somerton and Australia for this man. If we suppose he had fathered a son with Jessica Thomson, can we readily dismiss that he could have fathered other children with others in his homeland in Russia and the Caucasus, or elsewhere? Is the "father" being referred to in the code actually in reference to one or more other children he may have fathered before arriving in Australia? How about his own parents and relatives? Did they survive the two world wars and the revolutionary period and turmoil in the Soviet Union or anywhere else he was from?

Did TSM actually know his own parents? This question may seem odd to raise and entertain, but would it be possible to consider that he himself was raised out of a wedlock, conceived unplanned, of parents who perished in one situation or another, their child being adopted? Was he himself adopted or raised in an orphanage, for instance? If Robin Thomson found himself in a similar situation of fathering a child who he and his partner or wife had to give up for adoption, if we suppose that TSM himself had fathered a son he was unable to raise for health or economic reasons, why not consider that TSM himself was a result of similar circumstances, explaining why no one ended up searching for him and identifying him?

We do not have to consider the above to be an alternative story since one can accommodate it also with the common story assumed to have taken place in Adelaide, South Australia. If the DNA results prove his connection to a son born in Australia, in other words, we can also still expand the story to consider what TSM was doing for four decades before his passing in Australia.

A case in point that one can explore as a start is the life story of Anatoliy Vartanian, a legendary Lezginka dancer and teacher of dancing from Dagestan, living in Brooklyn, NY, today.

He must be aged about 85 now (in 2021), having been born in 1936, his fans having celebrated his 60th in 1996. He was raised in an orphanage in Makhachkala, the capital city of Dagestan, on the shore of the Caspian Sea. A talented dancer and dedicated teacher, with a voice that is heart-piercing as judged from even the short clips from his younger years, in his resume he has having danced for Nikita Khrushchev, Fidel Castro, and the Russian cosmonaut who was the first to round the Earth in spaceship, Yuri Gagarin. The mesmerizing brief clips of his voice and dances, and heartfelt expression of love for teaching, as found on YouTube are telling of someone whose life was dedicated to his Caucasian mountain culture and dances. Dancing for him was not just a hobby, he lived and is still living and teaching it.

The Somerton Man was of an age preceding him. When he was born in 1936, TSM would have been about 30 years old. If TSM was a serious folk dancer, among other involvements, from the Caucasus, perhaps Mr. Vartanian would know or have heard about such a man who vanished in the 1940s from the scene during his trips abroad. Such a line of inquiry would be also worthwhile to pursue for those interested in taking up the task and are close enough to him to ask, if he wishes to share his life's story growing up in an orphanage, if we manage to somehow detach ourselves from the Eurocentric habits of looking for a traditionally defined "ballet dancer" for TSM's identity.

Perhaps the dancing teacher's students in Brooklyn, NY, being close to him in body and spirit, can help ask their teacher more about his childhood background and ask if he remembers anyone resembling TSM's profile in the past, one who was perhaps named or known as Mr. Aiaqçi or аиакчи.

And here[85] is a clip "The Caucasian Sensation," in his and their own voices and lives. For further information, visit here[86].

17. Why Did It Take So Long to Solve the Puzzle?

The Somerton Man case was not about a murder, nor about a spying intrigue. It was a tragic, mysteriously played out love story of a terminally ill patient, acted out in a deliberately mystifying way, in relation to his silent dance partner.

The existence of the code was already confirmed just a few months after TSM's death. The information needed for its deciphering, as being reported by OKCIR for the first time, given the 'Tamám Shud' key, was already available from the very beginning and the case could have been solved, more or less, in a timely way. It actually took less than two months for OKCIR to decipher the code. Yet, it took more than seventy years to solve it, more broadly speaking. So, the long time it took to do so can also be itself regarded as a legitimate fold of the mystery.

Why did we not think that a transliterated 'Tamám Shud' from Persian may indicate that the code was similarly a transliteration from Arabic using Arabic alphabet? Why some of you reading these lines may not be still taking this seriously, even as a possibility?

While these aspects of the mystery may be regarded as "subjective" matters that should not enter the "objective" and "scientific" rigors of our investigations in our academic classrooms and laboratories, The Somerton Man case in fact offers us an excellent example of and illustration for how our still Newtonian outlooks in the sciences and aspiration for subjectless "objectivities" can go wrong by pretending that observers can simply delete themselves and their observation from the realities they observe, aspiring to be "objective" in an impossibly subjectless way.

The findings of the quantum sciences have indeed shown that the observer is always, inevitably, a part of the object he or she is observing, and objective and subjective realities can never be dualistically separated from one another, because the world is itself a substance characterized by inseparability. But we still continue trying to relegate the quantum world to the microscopic realms only, "shutting up and calculating" in our macroscopic social and academic spacetimes presumed to still follow the Newtonian laws, more or less. In other words, it is only our own continued Newtonian chunky way of seeing reality that leads us to limit our quantum sciences to the microscopic world, not observing the same happening in our macroscopic social realities, including how we go about decoding our Somerton Man enigmas (see here[87]). It is the Newtonian lens of seeing reality in a chunky way that allows us to juggle billiard balls of Australia but not of the Caucasus, of European languages but not of Arabic, of hard sciences but not the social sciences or the humanities.

Perhaps the most important explanation for why it took so long to solve the puzzle is our Eurocentrism. If you watch the clip about Anatoliy Vartanian, you can learn an important lesson from his first student when he says those in the U.S. (and presumably also Australia) know very little about Lezginka, and about *his* homeland. Even in a case that clearly involved Persian poetry, and transliteration using Arabic alphabets (in FitzGerald's case for Persian words), we did not seriously entertain the idea that TSM could actually be ethnically Arab and/or his code could be written in an Arabic transliteration environment. We felt the languages we choose to decode the code must be European, 'Tamám Shud' being just an exotic side-show to TSM's "Australian" mystery.

If you wish to learn something from The Somerton Man case, it is that the world is not limited to Australia or the West, but it encompasses, well, the world. If you find yourself still reluctant to even consider that the code is written in an Arabic transliteration environment, while knowing that 'Tamám Shud' was in fact a transliteration from Persian using Arabic alphabet, you may actually be able to observe in yourself Eurocentrism in progress, if you have the eyes for it.

A mind that looks for a ballet dancer in the West may tend to dismiss or not even entertain the possibility that an acrobatic Lezginka dancer from the Caucasus mountains has as much right to having high strong calf muscles, v-shaped body contours, large strong hands, and to having been wearing pointed dancing shoes as those worn on your French or Australian ballet stages.

Even though Omar Khayyam's Persian poetry are freely translated into English, the possibility that a code can be an Arabic language transliteration may be found to be too "exotic" to solve an "Australian puzzle," regarded as a "remote" and unserious possibility, perhaps even laughed at in public or private, such as when someone with a non-Western name contacts you or writes this report to suggest such a possibility.

If you think The Somerton Man case is something "out there" for you, to be curious about and solve, if you wear your quantum science hat more open-mindedly you will find oddly that you are The Somerton Man yourself. If you are reading these words, you have already become entangled with his life and enigma, whether for a month, or for a few years, or even decades. So, solving it should also include your being self-reflective and self-aware about how you have gone about solving, or not, the puzzle.

Hypnotic conditioning does not have to involve pendulums. Even a Somerton Man's code can replace the device. All it takes for a hypnotic process to unfold is a simple object or message, a willing subject, and their repeated, regular exposure to one another, in which deep curiosity can play a key part. Whether The Somerton Man intended it as such, his case offers us an opportunity to learn how we have been, knowingly or not, subject to hypnotic conditioning for years and even lifetimes. And such hypnotic conditioning also includes having developed a habit of thinking that our Somerton Man cases are just Australia's or the West's to solve, and not one that should encompass all humanity.

We find it more exciting to find a DNA traced to an American president than to a Lezgi dancing, Arabic-speaking ethnic minority from a Russian region, or to a simple migrant, terminally ill, who contemplates suicide despite having feelings for his ex-lover and certainly for his son.

Being a "Russian" would not mean to us that the spy could also be ethnically Arab, even though we find it "exotic" to have a mystery in our hands involving "Persian" poetry with an "Arabic" dressed and Orientalized lady with a funny hat adorning its pages as found on the copy gifted to Boxall. It is either A, or non-A, TSM could not be at once a spy, a lover, a Caucasian dancer, an ethnic Arab, a Russian, a poet at heart, and a terminally ill man wondering how to cope with not raising his child, or at least seeing and holding him for the last time on his last day.

OKCIR, which has devoted much time in recent years to exploring riddles in the sciences and Khayyami studies, finds in the Somerton Man's case puzzle and its resolution important parallels and lessons to learn; in fact, the difficulties with solving the Somerton Man case offer a glimpse into a much wider difficulty with solving other long-standing social and scientific problems.

When an enigma remains unsolved, it takes a life of its own, becoming an entertainment industry. Egos begin to grow and flourish around the case; so the investigation ends up possessing investigators instead. The puzzle is assumed to be "out there" only and not also "in here" in the attitudes we ourselves maintain in solving an Australian case in an Australian way. We do not even entertain the possibility that the very reason we have not been able to solve our Somerton Man puzzles through our universities has something to do with our proudly celebrated university and scientific procedures being in the wrong.

Science (and Khayyam's legacy) was supposed to be about doubting taken-for-granted beliefs and structures of thinking, about taking self-critical thinking seriously, and not about forever cherishing "quantum enigmas" or "FitzOmar" cults and attachments. TSM and Jessica Thomson, having been left-leaning, actually can teach us and Australia something here about being self-critical in how we go about understanding and solving our social issues and personal troubles. Actually, the Somerton Man case offers serious students and scholars of the sociological imagination a sad but wonderfully instructive case where the dualism of personal troubles and public issues just simply faded away in favor of the simultaneity of the two sides—how personal troubles, even of an unknown lone man dead on the beach can become at once global public issues, and vice versa, how a global public issue and mystery can become our everyday personal troubles and everyday concerns (see here[88]).

Identities, emotions, and attentions become entangled with such cases to such a point that even when some try to solve it with earnest, they end up not being taken seriously, instead treated impersonally as just another statistic in a long list of failed attempts. It may then appear to be more entertaining to continue the riddle and enigma despite new reasonable findings, since it attracts more media attention, and feeds into our aspirations to be more and more profiled in mass media.

The Somerton Man case is not only a tragic and mysterious love story; it also tells a migrant's story in the shadow of a devastating world war. Jessica Thomson's involvement in the case is telling of the silent yet lifelong commitment of a critically-minded socialist-leaning woman from Australia, having a mind of her own, sticking by her social and love principles to the end in relation to a man whom she loved but could not marry and depend on for raising their child, yet devoted her life to raising the child the best way she could in the secrecy of her long life, avoiding public attention to live her life the way she and The Somerton Man imagined for their son to live—cultivating his talents toward becoming a creative dancer himself in the Australian Ballet.

However, there is also something refreshing in how Australia has gone about solving this puzzle, both institutionally and in terms of the personal lives and efforts of those in Australia and Adelaide who have done their best to solve TSM's mystery. The continued passion of those in Australia who personally as well as institutionally found themselves intrigued by and interested in putting to rest the soul and identity of a migrant man who tragically died on their shores is also telling of what positive can result when personal troubles and public institutional issues and interests are perceived as joined in order to solve long-standing human riddles. Without their efforts and all their contributions this report itself would not have been motivated and researched in trying to decode this other mysterious DNA lettering left behind, still faintly beating the heart and mind of the Somerton Man.

Truly scientific spirit requires questioning not only others', but also our own, biases as investigators, scientists, and observers situated in the West, including Australia. Arabic is also a legitimate possibility for a code's language. Ballet dancing does not have to take the form of what you find in your European theaters; in fact they too started on pastures, and high mountains, by ordinary folks such as The Somerton Man and his ancestors. Migrants do fall in love with their new homeland sweethearts. They can also be quite romantic, poetic, and sophisticated in their creative thinking and sensibilities, even when contemplating committing suicide due to terminal illnesses.

Russian and Australian socialist-minded folks can also suffer from long-term and terminal illnesses, poetically expressive about how to cope with holding, or sadly not, their newborn children in arms and kissed for the last time on their last day. DNAs are not found just in bodies, but also in minds and hearts as congealed in the form of a supposed "code," for which "pure objective sciences" and the most sophisticated statistical tools can be insufficient for the unriddling needed. Such decoding requires a different scientific method, one that is not itself chunky but is transdisciplinary and transcultural in its approach, in which the sciences, social sciences, and humanities, are all considered to be equally necessary across the imperially imposed geographical, disciplinary, and departmental, borders also drawn up behind closed doors in world wars.

Codes do not have to have formal, either A or non-A, logical structures. They don't have to be written in just one language. They don't have to avoid medical terms and labels given to patients who do have their own proper names, still having feelings for a lady not married and a son not raised. Chunky, fragmented, Newtonian, either/or thinking, and genetic DNA decoding can never capture the subtleties of Somerton Man suicide note poetics. Codes can be poetic, each word having endless meanings, intended or not. Barley plants can have connections to Digitalis plants, and such poisonous plants (and many others) can also be known in traditional medicine to those coming from the Caucasus mountains, where in fact they originated from (see here[89]).

Large strong hands can have connections to strong calf muscles in acrobatic Caucasian dances. Name tags may have already been removed from used clothing affordable by a poor migrant father who was trying to look the best he could for his future son on a publicly chosen Somerton Park beach death-bed, *a la* George Marshall. Solving long-standing puzzles such as The Somerton Man's case do not have to be hampered by Arabophobias, Iranophobias, Islamophobias, or Russophobias, or other overt or subtler forms of Xenophobia and Orientalism, even if TSM is found to be neither ethnically Arab nor religiously Muslim, nor broadly Russian.

The true resolution to the enigma of The Somerton Man requires a willingness to question our own Eurocentricities that have actually been at the root of our many world wars, and are still ongoing. It requires humbleness in accepting that human troubles have always been transcultural in nature and their unriddling will always require transcultural and transdisciplinary approaches.

The simplest and most profound lesson The Somerton Man's case offers in a sociological imagination is that human problems can best be solved when the Newtonian dualisms of personal troubles and public issues are transcended in favor of their quantum superposition. So, kudos to all those closely investigating the Somerton Man case, especially over the recent decades and years, who broke out of the dichotomy, bringing marginalized everyday lives of unknown men and women of their land to the center of public attention and official concern and business, stitching back personal troubles and public issues into one inseparable whole, as how they should be regarded in the first place.

There is a reason the Somerton Man's relatives, beside Jessica Thomson who for personal and other reasons kept her distance, never came forward in Australia to identify the man originally. That is perhaps because he had no relatives in Australia, being a migrant, a traveling errand boy, by choice or not, apparently with a fit body and talent as a performance dancer. But then a whole series of people, both local and global, became his family, and that is the beauty of his sad artwork.

Celebrating the Somerton Man's life can therefore be a celebration of all migrants, known and unknown, to Australia and everywhere, since ultimately we are all migrants from the same place, all of us being of one same substance, as another Persian poet, Sadi, has reminded us.

18. Conclusion: The DNA of A Last Dance for A Lasting Life

The mysterious code appearing on the back page of a first edition copy of Edward FitzGerald's *The Rubaiyat of Omar Khayyam*—found several months following the death of The Somerton Man (TSM) in South Adelaide, Australia, on Dec. 1, 1948—was a suicide contemplation and planning note TSM was poetically drafting for himself in the form of a quatrain on the back of his copy of *The Rubaiyat*, giving a gist of why and how he planned to carry out a deliberately mystery-laden suicide as his last dance for a lasting life. The code was the creative DNA of his suicide plot.

It was written in the 'Tamám Shud' transliteration style—in this case not from Persian, but from Arabic with which he must have been either natively (likely coming ancestrally from the ethnically diverse and widely multilingual Russian Caucasus) and/or by training and education familiar with. In other words, the 'Tamám Shud' torn-out piece found in his fob pocket not only served as a lead to TSM's suicide note, it also offered the key to the code's deciphering.

The poem as TSM's personal note to himself, rendered seemingly as a mysterious code, originally served more as a 'Tamám Shud' style playful self-reflection than being intended for others to read and decipher, but on his last day, sadly not having had a chance to see his child and the child's mother for one or another reason, he ended up re-choreographing his departure in such a way that the poetry booklet containing the code could be found independently of her as a bread crumb for decoding his strangely publicized end of life performance. This ended up fueling even more the mystery behind his suicide, beyond what he had originally intended.

Therefore, to reiterate, it is hermeneutically very important to keep in mind the significance of the events that transpired on TSM's last day, mainly in terms of his not meeting Jessica Thomson that day for one or another reason. TSM's plot changed that day from what he had originally intended. Had TSM met her on his last day, giving his *Rubaiyat* booklet to her with the code on its back as a gift poem, there would not have been a reason to cut out the 'Tamám Shud' phrase to be inserted in his fob pocket before committing suicide. No one would have then found such a thing, leading to a *Rubaiyat* copy and the code on its back. His identity would have been even more unknown, no link to Jessica Thomson would have been suspected, and she would have been in a, so to speak, "passive evasion" mode just in case, per instructions given to her in person by TSM then (as inscribed also in his code's last line) and/or per prior understanding. TSM's poem would have then served merely as a farewell love poem to her with the booklet he was intending to leave with her and explain to her what it meant before he died.

However, since the meeting could not happen and he could not be sure of the reason, TSM changed his plot to how it eventually happened and is now known, with the 'Tamám Shud' piece in his fob pocket, booklet tossed into a car in despair for not having had a chance to meet her and his son for the last time, making it possible that others may knock on her door instead using that telephone number, now making an "active evasive" attitude on her part necessary, while not being concerned that she would be held responsible for his death given the code, and given she did not get involved in his suicide plan on that day.

DNA is a self-replicating matter that reproduces the basic structure of a substance. TSM's code metaphorically offers the DNA of his last dance performance in public hoping for a lasting life, one that was sketched amid his medical suffering. He was reflecting on his life, terminal illness, and expected imminent death, while reading the meanings conveyed about life and death in FitzGerald's translation of Omar Khayyam's *Rubaiyat*—a work of art that offered TSM a practical and proven example of how one can physically die but endure in human memory and spirit forever.

Not being native in English, being familiar with Arabic language and its alphabet, and being inspired by the idea of 'Tamám Shud' as a transliteration, he poetically plotted his departure in his own artful way. Putting the 'Tamám Shud' in his fob pocket was not just about ending his life, and did not just serve as a bread crumb to his booklet and to deciphering his poetic code. It also meant that the public performance of his suicide plot had finally ended, and a new phase of it had begun. Not only the "evasion" or "keeping distance" condition of the plot by TSM's dance partner Jessica Thomson allowed for the perpetual self-replication of the mystery, the oddity and seeming impenetrability of the code itself allowed for its global self-replication in the minds, hearts, and sensibilities of many across the decades.

TSM's Khayyam poetry book was not necessarily a copy she had gifted him as she did to Alf Boxall, so she may not have even known about TSM's copy of the Rubaiyat and how it looked, but having known him, and having become (like others) aware of the code on the back of TSM's booklet, she could have been in the best position to decipher to code for herself privately, being reminded again to "keep distance" about the case. And she did so to her last day as well.

TSM's self-reflective poem written as if in a code hinted at key information about the circumstances surrounding TSM's intended suicide due to what must have been medically considered at the time to be a terminal illness, one that he had been suffering from for a while. The second line (following the crossed-out line) actually offers specific medical information about the illness he suffered from, and the last line of the code specifically reveals how he planned to end his life by way of his own prepared poison being served poetically by himself as a Saqi and even by the person who would have been his suicide aid, Jessica Thomson, as a "wine-server," with a farewell final word to her (who was going to raise their child) to maintain distance from the case following his suicide.

The success of his artfully choreographed suicide plot fundamentally rested on her maintaining such a distance and confidentiality after his death, since the continuity of the puzzle was essential to his suicide plan's intended lasting impact. However, given that she ended up not being present at her home and involved on his last day, his wish for her keeping distance from the case following his death ended up becoming a self-fulfilling prophecy as well.

Jessica Thomson may not therefore have actually known of his plan on that specific day even though she may have been broadly aware of his terminal illness and his wish for ending his suffering by way of suicide. Their having had an affair and a child itself could have been a part of the plan, implying her realizing that she could not depend on him for establishing family and raising their child. But, not being sure of his plans and sincerity beyond their affair, she may have felt despaired about having trusted him, though they had kept in touch, given that TSM apparently had her recent Glenelg residence phone number. She may have even found herself unwilling to carry out her part of the plan as a suicide aid, given she still had feelings for him as the father of her child.

Given how events turned out on his last day, in the following months and years she herself may have wondered if the man and his death were known by those "higher than the level of local police," involving spying intrigues, since both TSM and she may have had spying or at least suspected as having critically socialist frames of mind and activities. All these misunderstandings then led to a series of events that further embroiled TSM's suicide in a lasting enigma assumed to be spying related, when strictly speaking it was not.

In any case, having learned that TSM indeed followed through with his suicide plan (despite any doubts she may have had since their affair about the sincerity of his involvements with her and his inability to help raise their child), out of caring for him she stuck by and respected TSM's obvious efforts to maintain secrecy about his suicide plot until the end of her life, not revealing his identity, thus fulfilling his wish to turn his passing into a lasting enigma.

TSM, knowing he was terminally ill and sadly not able to raise his child for health reasons and life conditions as a migrant, despite his love of life and being a trained folk dancer from the Russian Caucasus republics, chose to die amid a final mystery dance performance of his own choreography, in a dancing pose, with legs crossed facing what could have been the Caspian shores of his homeland, his right hand folded "in a funny way" at some point and raised as if dancing in another, with at least a tiny saliva at the corner of his mouth standing for the spit he wished to throw eternally at the terminal illness that denied him the rest of his life living with his sweetheart, raising their son.

TSM's suicide was not a celebration of suicide and death, but that of life. He could have ended his life in much more privacy and obscurity, and he did not even have to do so, was it not for his perception of a terminal end soon awaiting him for medical reasons. His "code" is telling of someone who "spits" at the fact that he has to end his life for medical reasons and sufferings endured, while being deprived of raising a son and living a marriage with his child's mother, at a time when the world was emerging from a world war. So, loving his life, and for the love he felt for dancing, he choreographed his departure as a dancing art on a public global stage, where he hoped his memory would also last, having been inspired by the example of Omar Khayyam.

19. A Dancing Celebration

To celebrate this deciphering of the Somerton man's code, it seems fitting to watch a few clips depicting Caucasian dances, two from Russia and the Dagestan and one from Iran's Azerbaijan. A quatrain from Omar Khayyam will bring this post to a close. The following links are also available online on the publication page of this report at OKCIR.

Following WWII, Russian victory and goodwill dance tours, including those from the Caucasus, were widely organized and performed throughout the West. Here[90] is a clip from a performance in 1955 in Paris, France. Another is a clip introduction from the Dagestan Lezginka State Dance performance which can be watched here[91]. The similarity of Robin Thomson's clothing as widely seen online (see here[92]) to the Dagestani dancers's clothing in the last clip linked above must be coincidental, but is still noteworthy. Is he unknowingly wearing TSM's Dagestani dancing shirt gifted to him by way of his mother?

The clip here[93] is a beautiful performance of the ancient Azeri dance Yalli by Azeri dancers. Further information about the dance can be found (in Persian) here[94]. In English the dance and its background are introduced here[95]. The last person in the row of the dance is traditionally called Aiaqçi (ایاقچی).

May the Somerton man, Mr. Aiaqçi, dance in joy again during his second burial in the arms of his new and hopefully newly found old families. The four-lined DNA code storing his heart and mind's story, hoping for a lasting life as sketched on the back of his *Rubaiyat* copy, proved resilient and telling despite the dusting of his body remains, the same having been proven time and again across the centuries by Omar Khayyam.

When before the angel's feet I crestfallen die,
And like a bird by the angel defeathered lie,
Beware, mold my clay into nothing but this Jug,
So I may live again from its fragrant supply.

— Omar Khayyam (Tamdgidi translation)

TAMÁM SHUD

Endnotes (Reference Links)

1   https://en.wikipedia.org/wiki/Tamam_Shud_case

2   https://www.youtube.com/watch?v=aJUZHIlteMs

3   https://www.eleceng.adelaide.edu.au/personal/dabbott/wiki/index.php/The_Taman_Shud_Case_Coronial_Inquest

4   https://somerandomstuff1.wordpress.com/2018/11/09/the-ultimate-guide-to-the-somerton-man-mystery/

5   https://www.amazon.com/Man-Suspicious-Death-Somerton-Beach/dp/0646544764/ref=sr_1_1?dchild=1&keywords=unknown+man+somerton&qid=1629585378&s=books&sr=1-1

6   https://www.nytimes.com/2021/05/22/world/australia/who-was-somerton-man.html

7   https://www.abc.net.au/news/2021-05-20/somerton-man-forensic-process-following-exhumation/100150868

8   https://translate.google.com/?hl=en&tab=wT

9   https://en.wikipedia.org/wiki/Romanization_of_Arabic

10   https://en.wikipedia.org/wiki/Shirvani_Arabic

11   https://en.wikipedia.org/wiki/Romanization_of_Arabic

12   https://en.wikipedia.org/wiki/Russian_Australians

13   https://mgimo.ru/upload/iblock/d49/d49a57f6f9db3c9f3e4e4016143532e2.pdf

14   https://omniglot.com/writing/dargwa.htm

15   https://en.wikipedia.org/wiki/Code_talker

16   http://mylanguages.org/arabic_romanization.php

17   https://translate.google.com/?hl=en&tab=wT&sl=auto&tl=en&text=%20إ تمّت&op=translate

18   https://translate.google.com/?hl=en&tab=wT&sl=auto&tl=en&text=إتمّت&op=translate

19   https://translate.google.com/?hl=en&tab=wT&sl=auto&tl=en&text=%0تمت%20إت|A
إتتمت&op=translate

20   https://translate.google.com/?hl=en&tab=wT&sl=auto&tl=en&text=%20%0مساA
سم&op=translate

21   https://translate.google.com/?hl=en&tab=wT&sl=auto&tl=en&text=%20%0مساA
سم&op=translate

22   https://translate.google.com/?hl=en&tab=wT&sl=auto&tl=en&text=%20%20سام
%0Aسم&op=translate

23   https://translate.google.com/?hl=en&tab=wT&sl=ar&tl=en&text=ست&op=translate

24   https://www.almaany.com/ar/dict/ar-en/ست/

25   https://translate.google.com/?hl=en&tab=wT&sl=ar&tl=en&text=%20
غاب&op=translate

26   https://translate.google.com/?hl=en&tab=wT&sl=ar&tl=en&text=%20
ستغاب&op=translate

27   https://www.almaany.com/ar/dict/ar-en/غاب/

28   https://omniglot.com/writing/dargwa.htm

29   https://translate.google.com/?hl=en&tab=wT&sl=ar&tl=en&text=اياقع&op=transla
te

30   https://osmani.ahya.net/english-turkish-dictionary-8235.html

31   https://tureng.com/en/turkish-english/ayak%C3%A7%C4%B1

32   https://en.langenscheidt.com/turkish-german/ayak%C3%A7%C4%B1

33   https://www.linguatic.com/en-GB/Dictionary-Lookup/ayak%C3%A7%C4%B1.aspx

34   https://www.google.com/search?q=%D0%B0%D0%B8%D0%B0%D0%BA%
D1%87%D0%B8&source=hp&ei=HOgGYaP3BpGl5NoP9c2ceA&iflsig=AIN
FCbYAAAAAYQb2LL5fLxG4qKEbyeaOK4toj0oUgRIF&oq=%D0%B0%D-
0%B8%D0%B0%D0%BA%D1%87%D0%B8&gs_lcp=Cgdnd3Mtd2l6EANQ2w9Y2
w9gwxJoAHAAeACAAVSIAVSSAQExmAEAoAECoAEB&sclient=gws-wiz&ved=0
ahUKEwij9duZupDyAhWRElkFHfUmBw8Q4dUDCA0&uact=5

35   https://www.google.com/search?q=%D8%A7%D9%8A%D8%A7%D9%82%DA%
86%D9%89&source=hp&ei=DCz8YPKMM-uk_Qb63obwDA&iflsig=AINFCbY

AAAAAYPw6HDew1FbCwhzLqoCaOuTi9DNJ-Syl&oq=%D8%A7%D9%8A%D
8%A7%D9%82%DA%86%D9%89&gs_lcp=Cgdnd3Mtd2l6EAM6CwguELEDEI-
MBEJMCOggIABCxAxCDAToICC4QsQMQgwE6BQgAELEDOgIILjoFCC4Q
sQM6AggAOgcILhATEJMCOgYIABAKEBM6CAgAEAoQHhATOgYIABAeE-
BM6CggAEA0QChAeEBM6CAgAEA0QHhATUKMCWO4MYLIRaABwAH-
gAgAGLAYgBzwOSAQM1LjGYAQCgAQGqAQdnd3Mtd2l6&sclient=gws-
wiz&ved=0ahUKEwjywpu5_fvxAhVrUt8KHXqvAc4Q4dUDCA0&uact=5

36   https://www.google.com/search?q=ayaq%C3%A7i&biw=1017&bih=1344&ei=6iz8Y
      K6vCvGk_Qbtnbi4Bw&oq=ayaq%C3%A7i&gs_lcp=Cgdnd3Mtd2l6EAM6CwgAE-
      LADEAcQChAeOgkIABCwAxAHEB46BwgAELADEAo6DQguELEDELADEMg-
      DEAo6CgguELADEMgDEAo6EAguEMcBEK8BELADEMgDEAo6BAgAEB46C-
      wguEMcBEK8BEJMCOgIIADoHCAAQsQMQCjoECAAQCjoKCAAQsQMQy-
      QMQCjoFCAAQkgM6BwguELEDEAo6BggAEBYQHkoFCDgSATFKBAhB-
      GAFQ0l5YsYsBYMSQAWgCcAB4AIABV4gB5gOSAQE4mAEAoAEBqgEHZ3d-
      zLXdpesgBD8ABAQ&sclient=gws-wiz&ved=0ahUKEwiuzOCi_vvxAhVxUt8KHe0
      ODncQ4dUDCA4&uact=5

37   https://translate.google.com/?hl=en&tab=wT&sl=auto&tl=en&text=ayak&op=trans
      late

38   https://www.vajehyab.com/?q=%26%231575%3B%26%231610%3B%26%231575%3
      B%26%231602%3B&d=en

39   https://tureng.com/en/turkish-english/ayak%C3%A7%C4%B1

40   https://www.vajehyab.com/?q=%26%231575%3B%26%231740%3B%26%231575%3
      B%26%231602%3B%26%231670%3B%26%231740%3B

41   https://www.definify.com/word/ayak%C3%A7%C4%B1

42   https://www.vajehyab.com/?q=%26%231575%3B%26%231610%3B%26%231575%3
      B%26%231594%3B%26%231670%3B%26%231609%3B&d=en

43   https://www.vajehyab.com/?q=%26%231575%3B%26%231610%3B%26%231575%3
      B%26%231602%3B%26%231670%3B%26%231609%3B&d=en

44   https://osmani.ahya.net/english-turkish-dictionary-8235.html

45   https://en.wikipedia.org/wiki/Ayaghchi

46   https://www.google.com/search?q=ayakchi&ei=pqkAYbnlEo7JtQatuZ7QAQ&oq=a
      yakchi&gs_lcp=Cgdnd3Mtd2l6EAMyBwgAELEDEA0yBwgAELEDEA0yBAgAEA-

0yBAguEA0yBAguEA0yBAguEA0yBAgAEA0yBAgAEA0yBAgAEA0yBAgAEA06B-
wgAEEcQsAM6CgguELEDEA0QkwJKBAhBGABQgitYrTBg_jNoAXAAeACAAW-
CIAaMBkgEBMpgBAKABAaoBB2d3cy13aXrIAQLAAQE&sclient=gws-wiz&ved=
0ahUKEwi50JflxYTyAhWOZM0KHa2cBxoQ4dUDCA4&uact=5

47   http://tazehkand.blogfa.com/category/3

48   http://zti.hu/sipos_gyujtesek/pdf/045c.pdf

49   https://translate.google.com/?hl=en&tab=wT&sl=ar&tl=en&text=أب&op=translate

50   https://translate.google.com/?hl=en&tab=wT&sl=ar&tl=en&text=%0ءملىA
ملى&op=translate

51   https://en.bab.la/dictionary/arabic-english/ءملى

52   https://translate.google.com/?hl=en&tab=wT&sl=ar&tl=en&text=و&op=translate

53   https://translate.google.com/?hl=en&tab=wT&sl=ar&tl=en&text=طبى&op=translate

54   https://www.almaany.com/ar/dict/ar-en/طبى/

55   https://translate.google.com/?hl=en&tab=wT&sl=en&tl=ar&text=pope%0Apet
er%20sampras%0Aportugal&op=translate

56   https://www.ncbi.nlm.nih.gov/books/NBK185329/

57   https://rarediseases.org/rare-diseases/polyarteritis-nodosa/

58   https://www.ncbi.nlm.nih.gov/pmc/articles/PMC2917831/

59   https://www.cedars-sinai.org/health-library/diseases-and-conditions/m/microscop-
ic-polyangiitis-mpa.html

60   https://www.hopkinsvasculitis.org/types-vasculitis/microscopic-polyangiitis/

61   https://www.hopkinsvasculitis.org/types-vasculitis/microscopic-polyangiitis/

62   https://www.ahajournals.org/doi/pdf/10.1161/01.CIR.3.4.481

63   https://pmj.bmj.com/content/postgradmedj/62/732/965.full.pdf

64   https://link.springer.com/article/10.1007/s12024-011-9290-1

65   https://www.almaany.com/ar/dict/ar-en/عتد/

66   https://pubmed.ncbi.nlm.nih.gov/33830207/

67   https://translate.google.com/?hl=en&tab=wT&sl=ar&tl=en&text=%0ملياA%0مليّاA

مَليَاAمَليَاً&op=translate0%

68　https://www.almaany.com/ar/dict/ar-en/مَليَاً/

69　https://translate.google.com/?hl=en&tab=wT&sl=ru&tl=ar&text=oi&op=translate

70　https://www.almaany.com/ar/dict/ar-en/مَلي/

71　https://translate.google.com/?hl=en&tab=wT&sl=ar&tl=en&text=اوى&op=translate

72　https://translate.google.com/?hl=en&tab=wT&sl=ar&tl=en&text=رغو&op=translate

73　https://www.almaany.com/ar/dict/ar-en/رغو/

74　https://www.almaany.com/ar/dict/ar-en/أب/

75　https://translate.google.com/?hl=en&tab=wT&sl=ar&tl=en&text=أبA0%
　　اب&op=translate

76　https://www.almaany.com/ar/dict/ar-en/أبد/

77　https://translate.google.com/?hl=en&tab=wT&sl=ar&tl=en&text=أبد20%
　　&op=translate

78　https://www.almaany.com/ar/dict/ar-en/عتد/

79　https://anemptyglass.fandom.com/wiki/Joseph_(George)_Saul_Haim_Marshall

80　https://en.wikipedia.org/wiki/Sadegh_Hedayat

81　https://en.wikipedia.org/wiki/Lezgins

82　https://en.wikipedia.org/wiki/Caucasus

83　https://en.wikipedia.org/wiki/Lezginka

84　https://upload.wikimedia.org/wikipedia/commons/4/46/Spatial_frequency_distri-
　　bution_of_different_sub-lineages_of_mtDNA_haplogroup_H.png

85　https://youtu.be/UV7LdCUrsnQ

86　https://www.schoolandcollegelistings.com/US/New-York/262517210548479/
　　Lezginkanyc

87　https://www.okcir.com/product/liberating-sociology-from-newtonian-toward-
　　quantum-imaginations-volume-1-unriddling-the-quantum-enigma/

88　https://onlinelibrary.wiley.com/doi/abs/10.1002/9781405165518.wbeos1673

89　https://en.wikipedia.org/wiki/Digitalis_ciliata

90   https://youtu.be/iW28jVKqg20

91   https://www.youtube.com/watch?v=vauxq1wypsM

92   https://www.dailymail.co.uk/news/article-3104185/Was-Somerton-Man-spy-
       fathered-son-Adelaide-woman-New-evidence-break-open-enduring-mystery-body-
       washed-beach-nearly-70-years-ago.html

93   https://youtu.be/-NhqdCfgGzo

94   https://azb.wikipedia.org/wiki/%DB%8C%D8%A7%D9%84%D9%84%DB%8C_
       (%D8%B1%D9%82%D8%B5)

95   https://en.wikipedia.org/wiki/Azerbaijani_dances

CPSIA information can be obtained
at www.ICGtesting.com
Printed in the USA
BVHW052330090223
658265BV00018B/374/J